Turning PROBLEMS Into Pro~~blems~~fits

Brandy M. Miller

© 2019 Brandy M. Miller.

All rights reserved. No part of this publication may be reproduced, distributed, or transmitted in any form or by any means, including photocopying, recording, or other electronic or mechanical methods, without the prior written permission of the publisher, except in the case of brief quotations embodied in critical reviews and certain other noncommercial uses permitted by copyright law. For permission requests, write to the publisher, addressed "Attention: Permissions Coordinator," at the address below.

Brandy M. Miller/40 Day Writer LLC

8150 N. Stemmons Frwy. Ste. G-1094

Dallas, TX 75247

http://writeyourbook.today

Ordering Information:

Quantity sales. Special discounts are available on quantity purchases by corporations, associations, and others. For details, contact the publisher at the address above.

Printed in the United States of America

Publisher's Cataloging-in-Publication data:

Miller, Brandy M.

Turning Problems Into Profits / Brandy M. Miller

p. 168

Ebook ISBN: 978-1-948672-25-2

Paperback ISBN: 978-1-948672-14-6

1. Small Business 2. Entrepreneurship. 3. Career Guides

First Edition

14 13 12 11 10 / 10 9 8 7 6 5 4 3 2 1

Other Books By This Author

How to Write an eBook in 40 Days (or Less!)

Creating a Character Backstory

The Write Time: How to Find All the Time You Need to Write a Book

The Poverty Diaries: Excerpts from the diaries of someone who's been there.

The Secret of the Lantern: A choose-your-path adventure for Catholic Kids

7 Secrets to Change Your Life & the World

I Wish I Could Draw Like That: Life Lessons from an Aspiring Artist

COMING SOON:

Writing Problems Into Profits

Turning Problems Into Games

Turning Problems Into Prophets

Making Prophets

Dedication

Dedicated to my son, Eddie, and his bride, Marissa. May you prosper and thrive no matter what life throws at you.

Table of Contents

Other Books By This Author...3
Dedication...5
Table of Contents...7
Introduction...9
Step 1. Find a Problem You Already Know How to Solve...15
Step 2. Discover Who Needs Your Solution & Why.............23
Step 3. Know Your Competition..29
Step 4. Connect With & Serve Your Audience.....................35
Step 5. Get Clear About Money...43
Step 6. Shed the Money Guilt..49
Step 7. Put Together the Roadmap to Success 59
Step 8. Select Your Packaging..63
Step 9. Decide On, and Set Up, Your Delivery System........67
Step 10. Let People Know What You've Got.........................73
Step 11. Make the Sale 79
Step 12. Exceed Expectations...85
Step 13. Gather Testimonials & Reviews...............................89
Step 14. Create Referral RewardS and Generate Repeat Business..95
Step 15. Develop Disciples..99
Step 16. Go Beyond the Roadmap.......................................103
Step 17. Follow the Roadmap To Millions In Months 107

Step 18. Prepare For Success..115
Step 19. Join the Human Development Investment Group..129
Case Studies..143
Recommended Reading...165
Reviews (and Feedback) Appreciated...................................167
About the Author..169

Introduction

> The greatest difference between the rich and the poor is not found in their bank accounts.
>
> Turning PROBLEMS Into PRO*fits*BLEMS

Turning Problems Into Profits

The greatest difference between the rich and the poor is not found in their bank accounts. The difference in money is a symptom of a much greater problem. Simply put: The rich know their value. They know how to mine it, refine it, package it, and present it to others in a way that allows that value to be clearly seen and appreciated. The poor do not.

It is that problem that this book strives to solve. It is my goal to help those who have been struggling with the weight of financial problems they don't know how to solve, and who feel depressed because it seems like they can never get what they need to get where they want to be in life, find the value that they have to offer and then learn how to mine it, refine it, package it, and present it to others in a way that makes that value easy for others to see and appreciate.

THIS IS NO GET-RICH-QUICK SCHEME

You are not going to get rich overnight using this strategy. It will not happen. It is going to take time and effort for you to develop the skills you need to succeed. You will fail plenty of times when you try to follow the strategies I'm suggesting. Those failures do not mean it is time to give up or that it will not work. They are signs that you are learning.

When you first began learning how to walk, there were so many things you had to do all at once in order to succeed that you failed most of your first thousand attempts. You had to get your muscles strong enough to support the weight of your upper body. You had to balance on both legs. Then, you had to balance on one leg while you moved that other leg in front of you. Then you had to learn how to shift your weight so your front leg could support the back leg as that leg lifted up and moved forward.

You may have been trying every day all day for months before you experienced your first success, but because you didn't quit and you didn't give up, you eventually learned to master the art of walking. Now, you take it for granted and it is so easy for you to do that you don't even think of it as being a problem.

Building your business will be the same. There are so many balls that you must learn to keep in the air that, like a novice juggler, you're going to fail at most of what you try to do most of the time before you get it mastered enough to begin succeeding on a regular basis. The steps I give you in this book are a shortcut that will allow you to focus on what really matters and begin to experience success earlier. However, they won't stop you from failing. You'll still have to learn to master the concepts and that will only happen by you trying often enough and failing as many times as it takes to get it right.

However, I do promise you that if you keep trying and you keep persisting, you will eventually experience success. How long it will take you before you experience that success is not something I can predict. It depends on how many of the steps required you may have already mastered in another area of your life that you can apply to this process.

Once you master these concepts, they will not only begin making a difference in your own life but in the lives of the people around you. I know because I've seen this unfold in my own life and in the lives of others, too.

THIS IS A STEP-BY-STEP SYSTEM

What I provide to you in the pages of this book is a system that will make achieving the success you dream of simpler. It won't make it easier. You're still going to need to put in the work. It will simply provide you a system for success that won't fail you or let you down. It's real. It's solid. It works, and if you work it, it's going to work for you.

You will need to invest your time and your money to getting where you want to be in life, but if you are willing to do that, this system will allow you to have everything you want in life without needing a college degree or a special license to do the work you're going to be doing. Your background does not matter.

If you've been to prison or you've made some serious financial mistakes in the past, it doesn't matter. This is your clean slate. This is your chance to take everything you've been through and put it to use benefitting other people.

Your story and your experience are all the credentials you need to prove that you know what you're doing. Your results are the evidence that what you did works. You know everything you need to know to get started doing the work you're going to be doing. You just need someone like me to show you the way forward.

WHO I AM

My name is Brandy M. Miller and I am a Communications Consultant for 40 Day Writer LLC and http://writeyourbook.today. I am also the founder and owner of Magnetic Leadership Training. In November of 2014, I wrote and published The Poverty Diaries. It was a collection of excerpts from my diaries during some of my worst moments in poverty.

I know exactly what it feels like to face problems so big that you feel you are standing at the bottom of a 20-foot-hole and all you have to use to dig yourself out is a tiny teaspoon. It's overwhelming. It's discouraging. It's frustrating. And it's depressing. You feel trapped, hopeless, and helpless to change things.

Turning Problems Into Profits

A little over two years after publishing that book, though, I stumbled into a business selling my solution to the problem of how to write a book to other people. I didn't realize at the time just how many other people there were who also struggled to write books and how much money people were willing to pay someone to help them solve that problem. Since then, I've made well over $75,000 serving people in need of help writing their books.

That may not be a lot of money to you, but to me it was a mountain I never thought I could climb. I made that money without paying a dime in advertising and, if I knew then what I'm about to teach you in this book, I could easily have made 20 times that amount. You don't have to believe me. I've dedicated an entire chapter to showing you how to leverage the power of your solution to make yourself millions in less than two years.

LET'S GET STARTED

Now that you know a little bit about me and why it is that I am qualified to be teaching you what I am teaching you in the pages of this book, it's time to get started. Time is one of the 2nd most valuable kinds of wealth there is, and you're giving me some of it today, so I don't want to waste it.

Step 1. Find a Problem You Already Know How to Solve

> You've solved at least 10,000 problems in your lifetime.
>
> Turning PROBLEMS Into PRO*its*BLEMS

Turning Problems Into Profits

If I'd have met my first client back in 2004, when I was still struggling to figure out how to finish my first book, I would not have been in the position to help her with her writing problem. I wouldn't have known what to do to solve her problem or what the results could be if she did solve that problem. I hadn't done it yet.

If I had helped her, I might have succeeded, but I would have felt like a fraud the whole time. I wouldn't have been confident in what I was doing and that lack of confidence would have clearly communicated itself to her in what I did and didn't do. My strength came because I not only understood the struggle to write, I had solved that problem so often I was actually in the process of developing a system that would help other people solve it, too.

THE POWER OF YOUR PAST PROBLEMS

You've solved at least 10,000 problems in your lifetime. Many of these things you have solved so often that you take them for granted and you don't even have to think about what to do or how to do it anymore. However, just because you can solve it easily does not mean that other people can.

You're looking for a problem you can solve that meets the following criteria: 1) Caused you a serious amount of grief before you figured out how to solve it for yourself; 2) You would gladly have paid good money if someone else would have solved it for you before you figured out how to solve it; 3) It is not a problem that most people know how to solve. It helps if it's something other people routinely ask for your help in doing so that you know for a fact that there are people out there who want it done for them.

When I think back on how much money I paid over the years for writing courses and books and seminars, it's hardly surprising to me that someone gladly paid me thousands of dollars to get my help writing their book. The truth is that 80-90% of people believe they have a book in them but fewer than 3% will ever write it. That's because most of them don't know where to begin or how to get past writers block once they do begin or even how to determine where the ending should be.

Your past problems, those problems that you routinely solve without having to think about it, are the source of your present fortune. They're just waiting for you to tap into them and begin mining the value out of them.

You know how to solve the problem and – more importantly – you know what results solving that problem is going to provide to the person who does what you did. I didn't know everything a book could do for you back then, but I did know that writing a book would change your life even if the only person who ever read it was you.

I knew it would lend you a confidence that simply could not be gained doing anything else. I knew it would open your eyes and cause you to change the way you saw yourself and the people around you. I knew, because that's what had happened to me.

I was able to close the deal with that first client of mine because I knew how to help her experience those results in a very short period of time. I knew how to paint the picture of what her life would be like when that book was written and she held it in her hands.

Remember this: People buy to get results. They want something to change in their life.

It's your knowledge of the changes that will come out of getting their problem solved the way you do it that makes your past such a powerful resource for finding problems.

CHOOSING THE RIGHT PROBLEM TO BEGIN

As I stated in the last section, you've already solved thousands of problems in your life, but not all of those problems are going to provide the right foundation for you to build the life of your dreams. Be sure the problems you know how to solve make you feel good when you solve them, are problems you find exciting to solve, and are problems you would happily solve for the rest of your life if you didn't have to interrupt the time you spend with annoying little habits like eating, drinking, or sleeping.

I technically know how to clean a house. I get no pleasure out of solving that problem for myself and only a marginal amount of pleasure out of solving it for other people. I'm not going to start a cleaning business because I would find that business something that made me grit my teeth every single day I did it. There's no amount of money in the world that is worth that kind of grief or aggravation.

The businesses I do run – magnetic leadership training and writing problems into profits – are things that inspire and motivate me. They bring me great joy and satisfaction to do because I know the difference I am making. I would write all day long every day whether anyone ever saw my work or not because it's something I love doing. Therefore, it is a great fit for using as a foundation of building my dreams.

Don't choose your problem based on how much money you think you can make out of it and then end up trapped in a life with lots of money but much misery at the same time. A girlfriend of mine did that. She built a multi-million dollar real estate business but she hated her work and she hated her business.

She eventually lost everything but she was happier and was freed to build a new business on a foundation of putting her art to work helping other people visualize their problems and challenges and find solutions to those. She is now happier than she's ever been and more financially successful than she's ever been.

TURNING ON THE PROFIT TAP

Once you start that first venture with that first problem, you're going to start seeing the power of what I'm teaching you. Imagine being able to take every single one of those past problems you've figured out how to solve and installing in those problems a faucet that would allow you to turn on the tap and have profits begin pouring out from those.

That's the true secret that the wealthy use to keep hold of their wealth even in tough financial times. They have at least 7 different streams of income flowing into their accounts. That way, if they lose one source of income, they have 6 more that are still supporting them until they can find a new one.

You have a virtually unlimited capability to create streams of income that will pour into your life until you have an ocean of financial reserves to call upon. If technology causes one of those sources to stop producing, you will always have new problems to solve that can replace it. There will never again be a time in your life when you do not have the means or the opportunity to profit. Once you master this skill, you will be unstoppable.

Step 2. Discover Who Needs Your Solution & Why

> To the group of people that need your solution, finding it will be an answer to their prayers.
>
> *Turning* PROBLEMS *Into* PRO*fits*BLEMS

Turning Problems Into Profits

Not everybody in the world wants to write a book. Not everybody in the world finds the problem of being unable or not having the time to write a book enough of a problem that they are willing to pay the price required to get someone else to help them with that problem. I found my first client because I was in the right place: a group for people who were looking to write books and I connected with the right person: someone who wanted to write a book but didn't have time to do it themselves.

The problem you choose to solve won't be something everyone needs to have solved. Not everyone in the world will find that problem so pressing that they are willing to invest their time and money to obtain a solution. To the group of people that need your solution, finding it will be an answer to their prayers. It may literally save their life.

WHO YOU WERE

To figure out who is likely to need it, you need to look for common threads that connect you to that audience. What is a trait that the two of you share in common? In my case, I found my first client because we were both interested in writing books. I was a writer and so was she, but she didn't have time to write her own book.

I like to figure out who to connect to by starting with a very broad group of people who share an interest, a hobby, a career, a belief, or a lifestyle choice that I've made. That gives me an instant way to connect with them and narrows down my list of probable suspects for who might need what I have.

WHAT THE SOLUTION DID FOR YOU

Consider the solution you have found. What did it do for your life? What were the positive changes that it made that you didn't expect? What were things you expected that solution to do for you that it didn't do? Did finding that solution cause you other problems? How is your life different today from what it was then?

It's important to be open and honest about all aspects of the transformation that happened in your life because of finding this solution and implementing it in your life. You want to be sure that the people you sell this solution to are prepared for its limitations and are given tools to help overcome or deal with any negative challenges that may come as a result of the solution.

WHAT THAT SOLUTION WAS WORTH

To figure out the value that your solution can bring to someone else, sit down and answer the following questions:

1. How much money would you have glad-

ly paid if someone would only have helped you solve that problem back when it was making your life the most miserable?

2. How much of your time was being spent on trying to solve that problem? How much money per hour were you making at the time. Multiply the time spent solving that problem by the money per hour you were making.

3. How many years did this problem take you to solve? Multiply answer 2 by this number and see how much time value in total your solution is worth.

4. How much stress was this problem putting on your relationships?

5. What was it doing to your health emotionally, physically, or mentally?

While those last two questions don't have an exact dollar figure to offer, they are just as important in terms of determining the value that your solution brings and its worth to the person you are offering that solution to.

For myself, I know I spent thousands of dollars in terms of time and money trying to solve that problem of not knowing how to get to the end of a book. That does not include all the money and opportunities I lost because I couldn't solve the problem.

Step 3. Know Your Competition

> *A healthy market has plenty of room for all kinds of competition because there are always gaps in the market.*
>
> *Turning* **PROBLEMS** *Into* **PRO*fits*BLEMS**

Turning Problems Into Profits

When my first client asked me that unexpected question, "How much would you charge to write my book for me?" I was unprepared. I didn't know what I should charge or what the competition was charging. I didn't tell her I didn't know. I pulled up a Google browser and typed in "How much does the average ghostwriter charge?"

I discovered the answer was $35,000. I went back into my chat and typed in "The average ghostwriter charges $35,000." And then I waited to see what she would do. I expected her to tell me, "No, thank you." But she didn't. Instead she said, "That's a lot of money. What would I get for it?"

I didn't know how to answer that question either, so I told her I would get back with her with a proposal. What I should have done is do my competition research and find out what other people were putting into their packages. Instead of $35,000, I made less than 10% of that because I didn't know my competition.

COMPETITION IS GOOD NEWS

One of the things I learned from one of my writing mentors, Vic Johnson, was not to fear the competition. Just because there are already 5,000 books on the topic of entrepreneurship doesn't mean there isn't room for one more. Actually, having a lot of competition out there is good news. When you see very few titles for a particular problem, that usually means there are very few people searching for solutions and that means you're going to have a hard time finding people to buy your product or service.

A healthy market has plenty of room for all kinds of competition because there are always gaps in the market. Maybe you offer the best widget in the world, but someone can't afford your price and so now there's a gap in the widget market where someone who produces the same widget but with less costly materials can step in and help those people.

Maybe your widgets work really well for people who are expert widget workers but they are tough for inexperienced widget workers to manipulate. Now there's a gap in the market where someone who produces a widget that is easier to use can step in and help those inexperienced widget workers get their work done.

Your solution may work for everyone, but it won't work at the same level for everyone which means there will always be room for other people to create more tailored solutions that adapt to the needs of another, smaller market.

GOOGLE AND AMAZON

Two of the best places to start your competition research are Google and Amazon. Obviously, part of what I do is help people get their books written so I usually start out on Amazon.

I type in the problem that the book I'm working on is designed to solve and I look for the top 10 titles that come up. It's a little harder to find the real results these days because Amazon shoves their paid placement ads at the top, so you want to be aware of that when you're doing your research. Google does that same thing. The top 3 results usually aren't the best results but are paid advertisements.

When I'm on Amazon, here is what I am looking for with those top 10 titles: their rankings, their categories, their reviews, their pricing, their page counts, what formats they offer, whether they self-published or traditionally published, who the author is, and when they released the book.

I pay the most attention to the reviews because that tells me what readers wanted that they didn't get and what they did get that they didn't want. It gives me a clear idea of where the gaps are in the market place. The pricing of my competition gives me a good idea for where my pricing should fall. The rankings tell me how many copies are probably selling per day so I know whether this is a popular genre or not. The categories they use give me an idea of the categories I should be using to help customers find me.

When you're doing research on Google, you do want to use the top 10 websites that come up after the paid advertisements as your base. You want to know what your competitors are offering, how much they are pricing their services at, what kinds of ways that they package their offer, and then go look and see if you can find reviews for that offer. You especially want to look for the negative reviews. What were people getting that they didn't want or not getting that they did want? That's where you can fit into the marketplace and carve a name for yourself.

STUDY YOUR COMPETITION

You want to get to know your competition well enough that you know what they do very well and you know what they don't do or don't do as well as you can. You want to be able to tell your prospects why your product is exceptional at handling the areas where your competitors are strong and how it compares in performance to the strengths of your competitors.

Knowing your competition this well will help position you as an expert in your marketplace. It will also give you ideas for how you could potentially partner with your competitors to offer something to their audiences that they can't in a way that would create a win-win-win for everyone.

Step 4. Connect With & Serve Your Audience

> *If you're a Facebook user, finding groups to join is easy.*
>
> *Turning* PROBLEMS *Into* PRO~its~BLEMS

If not for joining that group of writers who were trying to write their books, I would never have met my first client and would not have uncovered the system I offer you today. Having solutions to offer will do you absolutely no good unless you get out there and connect with the people who need that solution the most.

LOOK FOR GROUPS THAT SHARE COMMON TRAITS WITH YOU

If you're a Facebook user, finding groups to join is easy. You just type in the common traits you selected for your audience and you start searching away. Don't join more than 2-3 groups to begin with. You don't want to stretch yourself too thin.

I do also recommend that you get involved in groups in the real world. The digital world is not a substitute for face-to-face human interaction. You can build relationships a lot quicker if you can connect with people in person than you can online.

The trick is to look for groups that share common traits with you. If you're a mother, join a mother's group even if your kids are in their 60's. You can still make it work.

If you are a professional, join a group for career professionals. LinkedIn is terrific for that kind of networking.

LISTEN TO UNDERSTAND

If not for that first client of mine, I doubt I would ever have understood how powerful this technique is. She was so different from me that I didn't know if we'd be able to get along. We seemed to have few things in common.

However, my goal was to interview her to get her story out of her and so I was asking questions and genuinely listening to the answers, not to judge her or to respond to what she was saying, but to try and understand her and how she saw the world.

I put away my need to judge or to criticize and I just listened to try and gain insight into her thought process and her experience. Helping her with that book was literally life-changing for me.

As I opened up to seeing the world the way she did, I did see her flaws and faults and her mistakes, but I also saw her heart and her struggles. I saw her, not her titles or her labels, but the person she was behind those things. And in seeing her, I saw so much of myself in her that I couldn't help but love her.

When you listen to understand the way other people see the world, it's going to change your life for the better. You will gain a new perspective on life and you will begin to see things in ways you didn't know were possible. It's a very powerful strategy that will broaden your horizons.

Plus, that kind of listening affirms the value of another human being. People love to speak about themselves and their ideas but it is so rare for someone to be genuinely interested in their point of view and willing to listen to them that you will automatically become someone they like just by listening.

There's another benefit to listening this way. When most people talk to the people around them, they might as well be speaking Greek. They assume that people who use the same words they do mean the same things they do, but that's often not the case at all. Two people using the word love may mean very different things by that word.

When you listen to understand how another person sees things, you will uncover their meaning for the words they use. You will then be able to use that language when you speak to them. You will know what their hopes and dreams and fears and struggles are, and you will be able to speak to those things and show them how your solution can help them achieve their dreams and overcome their fears.

SEEK TO SERVE

I spent the better part of 36 years trying and failing to start a successful business. I did not have a clue as to what I was doing wrong when it came time to selling what I had to offer.

It was in the middle of listening to my first client's story that I started to get an inkling of what I'd been doing wrong. She told me that one of the secrets to her success was in serving the people around me. She said, "Every time I served someone else with a pure intention of serving them and not to gain, my business would begin to prosper."

I realized that service was exactly what brought that client to my door and it was service that led to every success that I'd had in life. If I wanted more success in my life, I needed to be more like a farmer.

First, a farmer knows that the seeds you plant today aren't going to produce fruit tomorrow. Every seed you plant has a different amount of time it takes between the planting and the harvesting. Some seeds, like tomato seeds, may see their first harvests in just 60 days. Other seeds, like a walnut, may take 5 years before you see the first fruits.

Second, the farmer knows that those first fruits from your acts of service may not produce much, either. It can seem a waste of the time you've taken when all you get is one or two tomatoes or a scant bushel of walnuts after 5 years of service. However, the longer it takes to produce that fruit, the more abundant the harvest when it finally reaches maturity and the longer it will produce returns.

Third, a farmer knows that just planting a single seed isn't going to produce much bounty. If you want prosperity, you have to find ways to plant as many seeds as you can as quickly as you can and to do that regularly.

Fourth, a gardener knows that just planting a seed isn't enough. You need to tend that seed, nurture and cultivate it, and keep giving it care and attention. Weeds can quickly overtake the seeds you've planted if you're not vigilant in watching over it.

That means just doing a single act of service for someone will eventually produce returns, but you'll get greater returns and get them more often if you are consistent in cultivating a relationship with the people you've served.

KEY STRATEGIES:

1. Join groups or organizations that cater to the kind of people you've selected as your audience.

2. Listen to understand what the people in that group are saying not so you can respond or tell them all about yourself, but to try and understand them and see how they see the world.

3. Look for opportunities to serve them, not out of intention to gain, but as a way of building relationships with them and learning more about them.

4. Cultivate relationships with those you've served.

TRUE FACT:

80% of people in any group or organization joined it to get something. If you're one of the 20% that are there to give something, you will not have to fight for attention. You will stand out from the crowd and attract attention automatically.

Step 5. Get Clear About Money

> Money is not evil.
> Money is not the root of all evil.

Turning PROBLEMS *Into* PRO~its~BLEMS

Turning Problems Into Profits

One of the biggest problems, one that is consistent across my life, is a struggle with money. As a kid growing up, money was blamed for every problem my family faced and was said to be the solution to every problem. "We can't [fill in the blank here] because we don't have the money."

It took me years and years to realize that money was not the problem in our household and it was not the answer to our problems. The problem was our money mindset. The solution to that money mindset was to get clear about what money was, what it meant, how it was gained, and what its place in our lives should be.

MONEY IS NOT EVIL

Money is not evil. Money is not the root of all evil. Scripture never said it was. The actual quote is "The love of money is the root of all evil."

When you love someone, you're willing to sacrifice your life for them. You will put them first above everything else. That's good. That's how it should be.

But it's not how you should treat money. Sacrificing your life for money is trading a nugget of pure gold for a mountain of fool's gold. It's a waste of your life.

Putting money before everything else in your life

is why so many people who built multi-million dollar fortunes got to the point where they had more money than they could spend in a lifetime, but so much misery to go along with it that they found no reason to live. Money just isn't that important in the grand scheme of things.

The truth is that money is the least valuable kind of wealth you can build. It can be lost, stolen, diminished, devalued, or destroyed at any moment. How sad would you be if you spent a lifetime building up a pile of money only to find that in your last moments of life, everything you'd devoted your life to gaining was suddenly worthless?

MONEY IS A TOOL

Money is a tool for trade and that's all it is. It is a tool that is designed to measure two things: how much trust you've earned that you can deliver a given result and how much commitment your audience has to getting that result.

Being trusted to deliver a result does not mean that you are a good person. A highly sought-after hit man may be 100% trusted to deliver on his contract, but that doesn't make him a good person. It simply means that you have developed a reputation for being able to reliably deliver what some people want.

Having lots of money does not make you a good

person any more than it makes you an evil one. It is what you do with the money and how you gain it that establishes whether your actions are good or evil.

When you look at money in this light, you owe it to yourself and to the world to become the single most trustworthy person on the planet in terms of delivering the result that you built your audience around delivering.

TREAT MONEY WISELY

I used to tell myself, "If I only had enough money, I would..." Now I know the truth. I don't need money to get everything I want. What I need is to take the value that is in me and use it to trade with other people for the things that I want.

Money is not an obstacle in your path. It is not to blame for your failures, nor will it save you from them. Money has no power except what you give to it.

If you want to know why you're always broke, look at how you treat money. Do you resent it? Do you push it away? Do you cling to it as if it alone could save you from whatever fears you have?

Think about how you would feel if someone treated you the way you treat your money. Would you want to hang around for long if you were treated that way?

Money makes a terrific servant but a terrible master. Tell money what you want it to do and it will do just that. Blame it for your problems and it will accept the blame and leave.

Push it away out of resentment of the responsibilities it brings with it and it will do what you ask and leave, taking the responsibilities with it as it goes. Cling to it out of fear and it will stick by your side but it does not float very well and you'll drown right along with it. Plus, if you're clinging to your money, it will never be able to go out and help you multiply your fortune.

Before you receive any money, decide what task it is you want your money to accomplish when it arrives. Create a plan for every dollar that is due your way. A friend of mine, Melinda the Income Organizer, helped me to understand the value of this. She suggested creating envelopes for every dream and every business investment and every debt that I owed, and then begin to plan the way I spent my money accordingly.

This strategy helped my husband and I to weather an economic downturn without ending up homeless again. I highly recommend you begin creating plans for your money and assigning it the tasks you want it to complete for you even before it arrives. That way, you're prepared when it arrives, and it doesn't have a chance to be wasted on things that won't help you build toward your dreams. It takes the emotion out of the spending.

Step 6. Shed the Money Guilt

> _The amount of money you charge someone represents their commitment to getting the results you say you can deliver._
>
> _Turning_ PROBLEMS _Into_ PRO**Its**BLEMS

Turning Problems Into Profits

Even when you know what money is, you can feel guilty for charging money for your solution. When you feel guilty, you'll find your confidence goes out the window and your ability to charge what you are worth is hampered. Moreover, your ability to get the other person to commit to achieving their dreams will be impaired and so you both are likely to lose out.

YOU OWE IT TO THEM TO CHARGE

In my second year of business, I wanted to charge higher prices for my services but the amount of money I was charging was 25 times the amount of money that I'd been charging. It was outside the price range of your average consumer.

I struck up a strategy where I would provide the materials for people to market themselves and help them fundraise for the money to pay me. I thought it was brilliant. It proved to be a business disaster. I learned an important lesson out of this.

The amount of money you charge someone represents their commitment to getting the results you say you can deliver. If they don't pay, they have no commitment to getting those results. You will do your work and deliver on your promises, but they've got nothing invested in doing their part.

As a result, the work you end up doing will be wasted and their chances of achieving the dream that they sought you out to achieve will go by the wayside, unrealized and unfulfilled. Getting their up-front commitment is something you owe them.

SELL TO SERVE THEM

You aren't selling them a solution to get rich. Getting rich is a byproduct of the service you're providing. You're selling them a solution so they will commit to getting the results they need and so they will actually be able to turn their life around. You owe it to them to get them to commit to their own dreams.

This is what sales ultimately is: An invitation to partner with you in helping them to achieve their own dreams. When you ask for money, what you are really asking them to do is to commit to their dreams.

You want them to do that. They want to do that. But they may need convincing on your part to believe that they are worth it and that this will work for them.

You won't be able to do that convincing if you're running around feeling guilty for asking them to commit. As long as you are truly invested in helping them to achieve their dreams, you have absolutely no reason to feel guilty for the money you charge.

WARM THEM UP BEFORE ASKING FOR BIG COMMITMENTS

Here's something else I learned during that process: Warm them up first before you ask for a major commitment from them.

Asking for a $25,000 commitment from someone who just met you is a lot like asking for them to say yes to a marriage proposal on a first meeting. It sounds needy and desperate, and nobody likes needy and desperate.

Instead, let them get to know you. Have them commit to something much smaller that doesn't take you that much investment on either part. That's kind of like going on a coffee date with them first so they get a chance to check you out and see whether they can see themselves working with you on bigger projects.

If they like you, they're going to send more work your way. Keep proving yourself and earning their trust. When your relationship is at its peak, THEN is the time to ask for the big commitment that they need to make in order to achieve their biggest dreams.

PRICE YOURSELF AT 10% OF THE VALUE

Remember the exercise I had you go through in step 2 of calculating the value of the solution that you offer? Add up the money you would have gladly paid and the time value of the cost of not having that solution and price your services at just 10% of that value.

You will know that your prospect is getting an incredible value and you will be equipped to explain to them in mathematical and emotional terms what that value is and why it is worth every penny they will spend to get it.

UNDERSTAND WHAT EXPENSIVE MEANS

You will encounter the objection that your pricing is too expensive quite often in your life as a business person until you start understanding what this is really telling you and learn to short-circuit that objection before it can even come up.

Expensive is a relative term.

To someone making $10 an hour, $1 is CHEAP, $10 is reasonably priced, $100 is expensive, $1,000 is way too much, $10,000 is astronomical, $100,000 is a dream, and $1,000,000 is beyond their imagination.

When you make $10 an hour...

It takes you:

6 minutes to earn $1

Turning Problems Into Profits

1 hour to earn $10

10 hours to earn $100

100 hours to earn that $1,000

1,000 hours (nearly 10 months) to earn that $10,000

10,000 hours (about 5 years) to earn that $100,000

50 years to earn the $1,000,000.

When you make $100 an hour...

$1 is nothing, $10 is CHEAP, $100 is reasonably priced, $1,000 is expensive, $10,000 is way too much, $100,000 is astronomical, and $1,000,000 is a dream.

It takes you:

6 seconds to earn $1

6 minutes to earn $10

1 hour to earn $100

10 hours to earn $1000

100 hours to earn $10,000

1000 hours (nearly 10 months) to earn $100,000

10,000 hours (about 5 years) to earn $1,000,000

When you make $1000 an hour...

To someone making $1,000 an hour, $1 is chump change, $10 is nothing, $100 is CHEAP, $1,000 is reasonably priced, $10,000 is expensive, $100,000 is way too much, and $1,000,000 is astronomical.

It takes you:

6 milliseconds to earn $1

6 seconds to earn $10

6 minutes to earn $100

1 hour to earn $1,000

10 hours to earn $10,000

100 hours to earn $100,000

and nearly 10 months to earn 1,000,000.

The Value of Knowing Your Value

Expensive is also relative to the return on investment someone expects to receive out of the money they are spending.

Turning Problems Into Profits

Someone making $10 an hour may decide purchasing $100 in lottery tickets is expensive but worth it because they are hoping to multiply that investment by at least 10,000-fold.

Someone making $100 an hour may decide that purchasing a $100,000 home is astronomical in price but worth it because they expect it to save them $1,000,000 over a lifetime.

Lesson: If you people are telling you that what you offer is too expensive, they are telling you 2 things:

1)   What you offer takes them 10 hours or more of work to earn

2)   They don't see how the money they are spending with you will bring them a return that is worth the investment you are asking of them.

This is why it is so critical that you take the steps I outlined in chapter 2 and KNOW YOUR VALUE. Whenever you encounter that "it's too expensive" objection, sit down with your prospect. Ask them to tell you how much they make per hour.

Ask them how long this problem has been going on in their life, whether it is days, weeks, months, or years.

Ask them how much they have invested, in their

estimation, in trying to solve this problem.

Take the amount of money they told you they make per hour and grab a calculator. Calculate first how many hours of their life they have spent struggling with this problem. Write that number down for them.

Then take their hourly rate of pay and multiply it by the number of hours they admitted they've been struggling with the problem. Write that number down and circle it in red. Explain to them that this is how much money they've already wasted trying to solve this problem their own way.

Now, circle in red the amount of money that they've spent trying to solve the problem. Tell them this is the amount of money they've wasted trying other people's solutions.

Add line number 1 together with line number 2 and tell them this is the amount of money that the problem has cost them so far. Tell them that every hour they delay in spending money on the solution you're presenting is another hour of pay they are burning through trying to solve the problem themselves.

Now, ask them how long they would like to wait before going ahead and working with you to solve the problem in front of them.

Turning Problems Into Profits

Then, sit back and let them think. Say nothing. Your nerves will tempt you to speak, but the longer you sit in silence waiting for their answer, the better. If they raise another objection, remind them of their dream. Ask them how many more days they would like to wait on making that dream a reality.

No matter what objection they raise, bring it back to their dream and how much waiting is costing them and how much further they are getting from their dream with their delays. Do not be impatient. Do not be desperate. Be confident and assured that you are doing the best thing for them in getting them to confront the problem and start to take care of it with your help. If they tell you they want to think about it, just remind them of how much delay is costing them.

They may try to talk you down in your pricing from what you told them it would be. Stand your ground. Be prepared to walk away. You are offering them an incredible bargain and they'd be a fool not to accept your help. Remember the words of my wise friend, Aimmee Kodachian: "Desperation leads to the wrong destination."

They need to make this commitment. The bigger the commitment they make, the more likely they are to take action on implementing the solution, and that is what you need them to do for them to get results and the rest of your business model to work.

Step 7. Put Together the Roadmap to Success

> Your prospects will buy from you when they have 100% confidence in your ability to successfully help them navigate from where they are in life to where they want to be.
>
> Turning PROBLEMS Into PRO*fits*BLEMS

Your prospects will buy from you when they have 100% confidence in your ability to successfully help them navigate from where they are in life to where they want to be. This is why people buy: to get those results.

WHY YOU NEED A ROADMAP

I was able to get that first client of mine because I had a roadmap to writing success that I used to show her how I could move her from not knowing how to write her story to having the story outlined and ready to begin in less than an hour.

My roadmap impressed her so much that she was willing to pay me that day even though we'd just met.

Your prospects want what you have, and that is why they are willing to pay you money to get it. They select what they buy based on their perception of your solution's ability to deliver those results. This is why they check your testimonials and reviews.

Since you are just starting out and you don't yet have testimonials and reviews to rely upon, you need to have the story of how you got from where you were to where you are mapped out so that they can see exactly how you developed the solution you offer and why you are confident it will work for them.

THE ROADMAP INGREDIENTS

Since I served that first client, my roadmap has changed somewhat. That's because my understanding of what makes people buy and what they really want has greatly improved. Your roadmap doesn't need to be elaborate. It can consist of these 7 steps:

1. The problem you faced.

2. The mistakes you were making that were stopping you from solving that problem.

3. The surprising truth you discovered that help you move forward.

4. The solution you discovered once you embraced the truth.

5. The struggles you had in trying to implement your new solution.

6. How you overcame those struggles.

7. The results you got after you discovered the solution.

THE MAGIC OF AUTHENTIC VULNERABILITY

If you're thinking to yourself, "I can't let them see my struggles. They'll think I'm weak and they'll doubt me," you couldn't be more wrong. Vulnerability like this, where you let people inside your journey and see you as a human being, will actually work like a charm to help increase their trust in you.

That vulnerability you are displaying shows a level of fearlessness that will increase their confidence in you, too. It will give them permission to open up to you and share with you their struggles and pains because they know you will understand and won't judge them for where they've been or what they're going through.

I want to caution you that authentic vulnerability does not mean dumping your problems on people's heads and leaving them there. It is not about you telling them where all of your aches and pains are and expecting them to listen and sympathize. They have their own aches, pains, and struggles and they don't need someone else adding to that burden. That is what I call emotional dumping, and it's not attractive nor is it healthy. It's verbal diarrhea.

Authentic vulnerability lies in sharing your struggles so they see that you understand them and then helping them find a positive message out of what you are sharing with them. It should leave them lifted up and filled with hope, not down and depressed.

Step 8. Select Your Packaging

Packaging is the way you present your roadmap to success.

Turning **PROBLEMS** *Into* **PRO**fits**BLEMS**

Turning Problems Into Profits

Your packaging needs to be selected to fit the audience you've chosen. It needs to be something that they can easily digest. Trying to present your roadmap as a game to someone who doesn't play games isn't going to result in either of you benefitting. Trying to present your roadmap as a book to someone who doesn't like to read will only frustrate you and make them bored.

You need to know your audience well enough to know how they are most likely to expect to receive the information you've got for them and the best way to present it in order to get them to consume it. This goes back to listening to them and developing that relationship with them.

PACKAGING SHOULD BE REFLECTIVE OF YOU

The way you package your roadmap should be reflective of you. It should use your unique combination of talents, skills, and gifts. It should be something you are excited about presenting to people.

For example, if you're a musician, you might be able to create paintings but they probably aren't going to be as good as your music will be and – as a result – the packaging won't show off what you can do as well as a piece of music can.

Now, I'm a writer. A lot of my content comes in written form. However, I am also a game designer and an educator, so I usually look for ways to package what I have to teach in the form of a game. It makes learning fun, and when people are having fun, they are likely to do it more often and stick with it until they master it.

If you're going to package your roadmap in a way that extends beyond your personal talents and gifts, it's best to partner with someone who does excel in that area and share the profits for what you create. You'll help them showcase their gifts and you'll increase your profits at the same time.

GET CREATIVE

There are, honestly, about a million ways to package that same solution – and that's good news because it means one solution can become a fountain of opportunities for you. I'll talk more about just a few ways you can flip this one solution into multiple streams of revenue to accelerate your income production in the final chapter.

Step 9. Decide On, and Set Up, Your Delivery System

Underpromising and overdelivering will wow customers.

Turning PROBLEMS Into PRO*fits*BLEMS

You've got an awesome roadmap to the solution, you know the audience that needs it, and you know the value that solution will bring to their lives if they accept your offer.

You've scouted out your competition and you know what they are offering and how they are pricing their goods, so you have an idea of where your package will fit into the marketplace. It's time to decide on what you will deliver, how you will deliver it, and what your customer can expect when it is delivered.

Thinking through the logistics ahead of time will ensure that you can test the service and make sure it is working before you begin making offers to your audience. It also allows you to calculate the costs of what you are delivering and how you are delivering it so you can be sure you are making a profit and not losing money on what you are offering.

WHAT YOU WILL DELIVER

Will this be a physical product or a digital product? Will it be a service such as coaching, consulting, a live event, or a class? You want to be very specific about what your customer should expect to receive when they pay money to you so that there is no chance of confusion on their part about what they should be getting from you.

HOW YOU WILL DELIVER

Will it be sent by mail or postal service? Will it be delivered by email or downloaded from a website? Will it be a combination of both? Again, you need to know this ahead of time so you can prepare your customers for how their package will arrive. This will give them a chance to alert you if there's a problem so that you have a chance to fix it.

WHEN YOU WILL DELIVER

In the beginning, you may be unsure about the length of time it will take you to complete an order. Give it your best guess and then multiply the length of time you think it will take you by 5.

It is far better to underpromise and overdeliver, even if it costs you business, than it is to overpromise and underdeliver. Underpromising and overdelivering will wow customers. Overpromising and underdelivering will lose customers. I've made that mistake before and it's never pretty when it happens.

I've noticed that overpromising is something that usually happens when I'm doing something for the first time or something I don't do very often. I tend to underestimate how long it will take because I don't know all the variables involved. I've learned that when I'm doing something for the first time, or something I haven't done very often, it's far better to be upfront about that and tell my customer "I'm not sure how long this will take me to deliver" and let them decide whether they can afford to wait than it is to tell them it will take me three weeks and have it end up taking me three months.

SETTING UP YOUR DELIVERY SYSTEM

This may require a little work on your part. However, I highly recommend you keep it as simple as possible. Rather than building a website in the beginning, create a Facebook page and drive traffic to it. It's easier to attract people to a Facebook page than it is to a website in the beginning, anyway.

You're going to meet a lot of people who are going to tell you that you need this shiny object or that one in order to be a success. The truth is all you need to do is know what you are going to deliver, how you are going to deliver, and what your customer will get from that delivery and you are ready to deliver. Don't let yourself be intimidated into overcomplicating things in the beginning.

Once you have regular business THEN you can worry about investing in a website. Those take a lot of work to put together and a lot more work to keep them up to date. You'll want to hire someone to help you with it so you don't have to take on that burden all by yourself.

Step 10. Let People Know What You've Got

> You should always be working to create a win-win-win for your customer, yourself, and the community around you with anything you offer.
>
> Turning PROBLEMS Into PRO*kits*BLEMS

Turning Problems Into Profits

Self-promotion may feel icky in the beginning because our society trains people to think of sales and marketing as being sleazy, pushy, or even underhanded. It should never be that way. You should always be working to create a win-win-win for your customer, yourself, and the community around you with anything you offer.

YOU OWE IT TO THEM TO SPEAK UP

Long before I learned how to finish a book, back when I was 23 years old, I found myself in financial straits so bad that I lost all hope for my future. My husband, who had taken a year and a half to find work, came home and told me he'd been fired from his job. I didn't have a job and rent was due that next week. We weren't going to have the money to make it.

I had a three-year-old son looking to me for support and I was sick to death of never having enough of anything. There wasn't a single person in my life that I knew that was really that much better off than me financially.

I thought to myself, "If this is all there is in life – just pain and hardship and struggle – I don't want it anymore." I wondered just how many pills in that bottle of pain medicine it would take to make sure I never woke up again.

Once I'd considered suicide for myself, another thought came to mind. "If this world is too hard for me, I can't leave my son to face it all by himself. It would be better to take him with me."

I think it was that last thought – the thought of killing my own son – that jarred me out of my depression and made me decide to fight for life instead. I'm so grateful that's how things turned out because there are plenty of times it doesn't turn out that way.

If there had been someone who knocked on my door at that moment to tell me that there was hope, that I didn't have to end my life to find a better future, I would have eagerly heard them out. I needed to hear it.

If your solution can save even one person's life, or change it for the better, you owe it to them to open up and share. It's selfish not to.

STOP MAKING IT ABOUT YOU

The biggest mistake people make when doing self-promotion is to focus too much on themselves and not enough on the hopes and dreams of the people they are promoting to.

Keep firmly in mind the things you know your solution can do to change their lives in a positive manner. When you know what their individual hopes and dreams are, be sure to keep reminding them of those and how your solution is going to help them achieve those hopes and fulfill those dreams.

Don't talk about what you want or why you want it. Your prospect doesn't care about that. They care about what your solution can do to move them closer to their hopes and dreams or help them overcome their fears and struggles. If you can focus on that, you'll win them over.

DON'T FORCE IT

You don't need to shoehorn your solution into every conversation you have. Don't force the conversation to happen. Wait for a time when someone is talking about their problems and you can step in and share how the solution you've developed worked to help you through a similar time.

Then drop it. Plant the seed and let the rest of the conversation water it. If they ask you about it, go ahead and discuss it. However, once you've brought up the subject if they don't ask about it, just let it go. Trust that you'll have other opportunities and remember that it is more important to listen to them and focus on earning that trust than it is to make a sale that day.

LOOK FOR OPPORTUNITIES TO SHARE YOUR STORY

Podcasters and vloggers often need guests to interview. Bloggers like guest posters because it cuts down on the amount of writing they have to do.

Make a list of the top 20 podcasts, vlogs, and blogs that share your target market. Do a little homework on these people. Find out who their target audience is, get the host or hostess name, the name of the podcast, and look for an idea for how your guest appearance on their show could fit in with what they discuss and benefit their listeners.

When you do reach out to offer, give them your reason for reaching out, what your solution does to benefit their audience, and 3 ways their audience could benefit from having you on as a guest. Then, follow that up with what you are willing to do to help them promote their show to the people you know.

If you have a social media following, tell them where that following is and how many people that includes. If you have an email list, include that figure, too. Let them know how many people are on your email list.

When you do get invited onto a show, show up on time, be prepared, and focus on making the host or hostess look good by being an interesting guest. Open up and let yourself be seen for who you are, where you are, exactly as you are. The audience will love you for it and your host or hostess will, too.

MAKE OPPORTUNITIES IF YOU NEED THEM

If you strike out with the bloggers and the podcasters and the vloggers, make your own opportunities. My friends, Wilnona Marie and Jade Dee of the And I Thought Ladies, are the masters of creating their own promotional opportunities. You can read more about them in the case studies. It's gotten them the attention of some high-level Hollywood executives over time.

Host your own podcast. Create your own blog. Record your own vlog. Invite authors who have books that might provide useful information to the audience you hope to attract to be interviewed by you.

Some bigger name authors won't, but most authors will be eager to get their name out there and will participate. Authors are always looking for opportunities to promote their books.

Don't use this to be overly promotional, though. Just a quick blurb about what you do and a link to where they can find out more if they are interested is enough. Let your content be the vehicle that spreads your message.

Step 11. Make the Sale

> *Nobody wants to feel like they are just a steppingstone to your next goal.*
>
> Turning PROBLEMS Into PRO(its)BLEMS

Now that you've got people aware that you're out there and what you have to offer, it's time to secure the prospect's commitment. You're going to need to make the sale for that to happen.

WHAT A SALE IS

It took me a very long time to figure out what I was doing wrong when I was trying to sell things to people. The mistake I was making was a simple one: I was thinking too much about what I wanted and not enough about what my prospect wanted or needed. I was focused on getting to my dreams, and I was viewing the prospect as a means to an end to getting what I wanted.

True fact: Nobody wants to be used. Nobody wants to feel like they are just a steppingstone to your next goal. If that's the attitude you carry into your transaction, your best prospects are going to run in the opposite direction. They're going to feel your manipulations and they are going to resist you.

The only people you will end up signing up are users who are looking to get what they can out of you. Those relationships won't be as profitable as the ones that come when you're invested in doing the right thing for the person in front of you.

I find that whenever I allow myself to forget this and start focusing too much on myself again, things don't go well. That's why I'm passing this information on to you. I don't want you to make the same mistakes I did.

A sale is an invitation you are making to your prospect for the two of you to partner together in helping them achieve their dreams. It's your offer to walk with them and guide them on the road to getting the results they want to achieve. That's all it is.

As long as you keep this in mind and focus on their dreams, not your desires, you won't struggle to make sales. You won't look desperate or needy or greedy. And you'll feel good about making that sale, too.

HOW I SPELL SALES

1. SEEK TO SERVE

Sales starts with service. You always want to think about how your roadmap and the packaging that you've put it in is going to serve your customers and help them achieve their dreams. You want to focus only on them and what you can do to help them.

2. ASK RELEVANT QUESTIONS

You want to ask them questions until you are sure that you understand the nature of their struggle and you have a good idea of what your product or service will be able to do to help resolve those struggles and get them where they want to be in life.

3. LISTEN TO UNDERSTAND

You're not listening to make a sale. You're listening to be sure that you understand what it is they need from your product or service and so that you can correct any misconceptions they may have about what it can do for them.

4. EMPATHIZE WITH THEM

Put yourself in their shoes. Think about what you would want or need or how you would feel if the situation were reversed. The more you empathize with them, the better you'll be able to persuade them because the more confident they will be that you genuinely care about their outcome.

5. SET PROPER EXPECTATIONS

When I first got in this business, I didn't bother to explain the process ahead of time to clients. I figured that they knew I was an expert and would trust me to do my job. I wasn't putting myself in their shoes and I wasn't prepared for the wrestling matches that ensued because of it.

I wasn't thinking about it from their point of view.

I didn't realize what I was asking of them. I was asking them to trust me to take them on a journey that they'd never embarked on before and so all the things I was doing seemed strange to them. They fought me every step of the way. It caused a lot of tension and friction between us because of that.

I now know when I am starting to work with a client that they need me to educate them ahead of time on what to expect along the journey to becoming a published author. If I don't educate them, they are likely to balk at the things I ask them to do and to wonder why things are taking so long.

Never mislead your prospect as to what they can expect from the roadmap. Prepare them ahead of time for any negative outcomes that may come as a result of the changes they are making to their life. Let them know, up front, what you can guarantee and what you can't.

PREPARE TO CONTINUE SERVING AFTER THE SALE

Never let the service end when the check clears the bank. Always make sure that they not only got what they paid to receive but more than they expected to receive at the same time. Be there for them every step of the way.

Turning Problems Into Profits

Be willing to answer questions and to be a go-to resource for resolving problems. If there are any – and I do mean any – changes in delivery date or method or if for any reason things go wrong, you be the one to notify them of the changes and what you intend to do to set things right.

Step 12. Exceed Expectations

> Going the extra mile means you work extra hard to be sure that every dollar they spend with you gives them way more than they expected to receive in value in return.
>
> Turning PROBLEMS Into PRO*its*BLEMS

Turning Problems Into Profits

This requires a little bit of forethought, but it does not require you to necessarily spend a lot of extra money to execute. Go out of your way to be sure that every person who works with you gets more value than they ever expected to receive.

Delivering great results is how you turn buyers into fans. Delivering results that far exceed expectations is how you turn those same fans into raving fanatics that don't stop singing your praises.

It's how you build a business that doesn't require dropping a ton of money into the marketing because the word of mouth reputation you gain moves ahead of you.

GO BEYOND MEETING THE KNOWN NEED

When you walk into a restaurant, you are focused on getting one need met. You want your stomach filled and your hunger to go away. Maybe you're thirsty, too, so you want a drink with that. If that's all the restaurant does for you for the money you pay, you will accept that. You will appreciate that. But you won't rave about it.

Hunger and thirst are the needs that drive you into the restaurant. The result you are looking for is something that tastes good and keeps the hunger pains away for a few hours. As long as it does that, you'll walk away a satisfied customer and you might even come back. But you won't remember it. You won't think to tell other people about it. You got exactly what you expected and nothing more.

However, if that restaurant owner greets you by name and treats you like you're one of the family, if they make you feel like you belong and they ensure that you feel like you're important, you're getting more than just those base needs meet and you are going to remember that experience. It's going to stick with you and you're probably going to become a fan of that restaurant.

People are multi-dimensional beings with many needs. The more needs your product or service can meet, the better the value your customer will feel they've gotten and the more likely they are to not just revisit your place of business but to spread the word about the exceptional experience they had.

HELP THEM GET MORE, DO MORE, OR MAKE MORE FROM WHAT THEY PURCHASED

In addition to working to meet those additional needs they have, think about ways that your customer could get more, make more, or do more with what they purchased. How else can the product or service you delivered be put to use for their benefit? If you include an instruction sheet with what you've delivered that shows them how to make the most of what they've purchased, they're going to not only be impressed but they will put you at the top of their list of people to contact the next time they need something.

Going the extra mile means you work extra hard to be sure that every dollar they spend with you gives them way more than they expected to receive in value in return. The minute you forget this, that's the minute your business will start struggling and you'll find yourself having to drop prices or pull gimmicks just to get people in the door.

If you stick with this philosophy, you won't have to worry about lowering your prices. People will find the service you deliver so valuable that they will go out of their way to give you the money no matter how much you are charging because they know that every dollar they invest with you is going to come back to them 10 or even 100 times over.

Step 13. Gather Testimonials & Reviews

> People do not trust the things a company says about itself but they do trust what other people say about that company.
>
> Turning PROBLEMS Into PROfits BLEMS

Turning Problems Into Profits

People do not trust the things a company says about itself but they do trust what other people say about that company. That's what makes testimonials and reviews from satisfied customers so powerful. It lends credibility to the promises you are making and says that you know how to deliver.

FOLLOW UP IMMEDIATELY AFTER YOUR PRODUCT OR SERVICE IS DELIVERED

The first time you should follow up is right after you've delivered whatever it was you promised to deliver. Ask them to be sure they enjoyed what they received and to ask them how their experience was and if anything could have been done better.

If you get some critiques, take those to heart. Think about what you could do to remedy that problem and then take action on it so that the next time it doesn't happen that same way.

TESTIMONIALS ARE POWERFUL

If someone emails you positive feedback, ask for a testimonial. If you can get a 5 minute interview with them about their experience through an internet conference call or a video interview, that's best. It proves to the person listening to the testimonial that this is a real person saying these real things about you.

ASK IF YOU CAN CREATE A CASE STUDY WITH THEM

When you find yourself with the perfect storm of incredible results plus a glowing testimonial or review, it's time to ask if you can use their situation to create a case study for your website. Case studies are detailed examinations of what you did and how you did it. They are a powerful tool for showing prospective customers how things could be if they hired you to help them.

Do not make a case study unless you've asked for permission first, though. Some customers don't want their name and brand all over your website and you'll need to respect their privacy.

HANDLING NEGATIVE FEEDBACK

I'll be honest. The first negative review I got of my first published book was absolutely devastating. I chewed over that negative review for months. However, rather than stopping me from continuing to write, I let it motivate me to figure out what I could do to improve.

If you're in business long enough, you're going to have at least one unsatisfied customer. Sometimes it will legitimately be no fault of your own. In that case, look at what went wrong and see what you can do to formulate a backup plan that would allow you to avoid the circumstances that led to this failure.

Sometimes it will be because you made a mistake. In which case, own your mistake and take some time to let your clients and customers know what you have done to ensure a mistake like that never happens again. Don't excuse yourself, rationalize the situation, or justify your behavior. Just own it and make sure you put a plan into place so it doesn't happen again.

BE GENTLE WITH YOURSELF

Mistakes are going to happen in life and in business. You're learning how to run a business, and that takes time. Be gentle with yourself and don't beat yourself up for every failure. Just make sure you learn from it and try your best not to repeat those same mistakes.

Don't be afraid of negative feedback. Even if things didn't go well and they tell you that straight out, it gives you a chance to fix things and make them right. You can put a plan into place to ensure that you do better the next time.

HANDLING ANGRY CLIENTS OR CUSTOMERS

It is worth doing everything in your power to satisfy an angry client or customer. The price of one single angry customer is a hundred people being told to stay away from you and your business.

That's way more business than you can afford to lose.

The first step to handling them is to remember that chances are good they aren't actually angry at YOU. They are angry about the situation and their anger is being directed AT you because it has nowhere else to go. They want you to fix it.

The second step is to stay calm. Math teaches us a powerful lesson about dealing with a negative situation: If you add more negative to it, you're not going to make it more positive. If they are angry, stay calm and reassure them that you would be just as upset as they were if the situation were reversed. Put your empathy to use here.

Try to find out from them the details of what happened and how it happened. Then, reassure them that you will do everything in your power to ensure a satisfactory resolution. Put together a detailed plan for correcting the problem and then be sure to share it with them.

Most people will be willing to give you a second chance if they believe you are sincere in your attempts to make things right. However, don't blow that second attempt. Once is a mistake. Twice is a pattern.

Step 14. Create Referral Rewards and Generate Repeat Business

> By rewarding referrals and repeat business, you encourage your customers to spread the word about your business and to come back for more.
>
> Turning **PROBLEMS** Into PRO*its*BLEMS

Turning Problems Into Profits

Referral rewards aren't bribes. They are gifts of appreciation for the consideration given by those who have worked with you in the past. By rewarding referrals and repeat business, you encourage your customers to spread the word about your business and to come back for more.

REWARDS NEED NOT BE MONETARY

It is not necessary to pay them money for the referrals and repeat business. Small discounts, extra services, or any manner of clever ideas can be put to use in creating your reward systems. What matters is that the reward be valuable to those that receive it.

One idea for a reward is to give anyone who refers someone to you a group coaching session with you on some topic of interest to them. Another is to give them a discount on their next package with you.

Whatever you decide to do, be consistent in how you do it. People do talk and you don't want to risk offending someone by offering something of incredibly high value to one and of incredibly low value to another.

REPEAT BUSINESS IS INVALUABLE

It costs you a lot of time and energy to get those initial customers coming to you. Every time they come back, you chip away at that expense until eventually, working with them is nearly pure profit for you. It pays to work hard to keep those customers coming back and loyal to you.

One of the things you can do is to offer special discounts on new services your repeat buyer might want to try if they've purchased so much with you. Another thing is to offer a special bonus that you normally would charge for (and that doesn't cost you a lot of money or time to provide) but to offer it free to them.

SYSTEMIZE YOUR PROCESS

Creating a system for these things keeps the emotion out of it and lets people know what to expect from it. One thing you can do to systemize it is to create an affiliate program where people who refer others get either a percentage of the sales or points that they can then accumulate toward extra services or special offers. It's up to you. Be creative.

For example, if you find this book amazing (and I hope you do) and you want to help me spread the word about it, follow these steps:

1) Take a picture of yourself reading the book and post it to your social media accounts

2) Leave a review about what you thought of

the book.

3) Join our Professional Problem Solvers Network on Facebook and make a post in the group with the links to your postings and your review.

4) I will invite you to join me on a YouTube interview where I dive into your story and help you launch your brand!

Step 15. Develop Disciples

> An employee is loyal to the paycheck, not the company.
>
> Turning PROBLEMS Into PRO*its*BLEMS

Turning Problems Into Profits

At some point in time, you're going to get too busy to do all this work all by yourself. Developing disciples – a system where you train your raving fanatics to do the business you've been doing – is a great way to make sure that the work gets done by the kind of people who have living testimonies to offer about what the program can do for them.

They get a license to use your system and you get a percentage of the income they produce in exchange for referrals from you. They get a business system they know works, you get the help you need to serve more people, and the people in need of your services keep getting the personalized attention and level of service they deserve. It's a win-win-win for everyone.

THE PROBLEM WITH EMPLOYEES

If you've ever been an employee, you know this to be true: an employee is loyal to the paycheck, not the company. When the paycheck stops or no longer satisfies, most of the time an employee's loyalty stops, too.

Furthermore, most employees are not business owners and are not invested in your company. They do not have a business owner's mindset and consideration of the consequences for how they treat customers.

They don't understand that every position in a

company is a customer service position whether it carries that title or not because they don't always directly see the impact how they handle things impacts the customer on the other end of the line.

THE ADVANTAGE OF DISCIPLES

Disciples are looking to build their own business. They are interested in learning from you best practices so that they can build a future of their own. They are, therefore, loyal to the service of the customer and they will often work harder than an employee would because of it.

This is especially true if you are being generous with the percentage you are giving them in exchange for the work they do for you. Let's say you set up 12 disciples who are each managing a portion of your customer list.

Even if each one is only paying you 10% of the revenue they make from the customers they service, you are collecting that amount times 12 people and you are only having to do as much work as it takes to oversee 12 people.

PROTECTING YOUR ASSETS

Now, before you go creating disciples, I do advise you to seek legal advice. You want to protect your assets from dishonest people trying to take it from you. As careful as you may be in screening your disciples, there will always be that one in the group that slips through the cracks and tries to steal your success from underneath you.

You will also want to make sure that you are in compliance with federal laws regarding franchises. The last thing your business needs is the headache of legal problems or to have your operations completely shut down and your assets frozen because you didn't take this step.

Step 16. Go Beyond the Roadmap

> *Real wealth is made of multiple streams of income.*

Turning PROBLEMS *Into* PRO**fits**BLEMS

Turning Problems Into Profits

This is where the real money starts to be made. Your roadmap is one product. What happens when technology comes along that makes that product outdated? You lose your income.

Real wealth is made of multiple streams of income. Diversifying the number and type of products and services you offer from that one solution is the key to building multiple streams of income without a lot of additional work to it.

GET CREATIVE

Look for additional products or services that you can offer to support or add value to your package. Let's say you wrote a great book. In that book, you talk about the perfume line you created and the business you built around it. Selling that perfume to the people that bought the book is a great way to add an additional stream of income.

Or, let's say that you create a course on perfume making and selecting the right perfume. You offer this to clueless guys who want to impress their girlfriends or wives. Now you've added another stream of potential revenue from that same book.

Everything you create has more than one way to make money from it. Webinars, seminars, coaching sessions, products that add value or extend the experience or enhance it are all opportunities to make additional money from that one source without doing a huge amount of extra work to make it happen.

ASK YOURSELF: HOW ELSE COULD I SERVE THEM?

Always be looking for new ways to serve the clients and customers you've got. If you experience repeat customer complaints or if customers routinely have problems using your product, examine it for an idea of something you could offer that would add value.

Think about what the next step is on the journey once they've got the results they need, what else will they need. It is thinking like this that led me to realizing that I needed to become a one-stop publishing shop for individuals interested in self-publishing. Becoming that one-stop shop to serve their needs led me to think about creating a television show for writers, and then to developing a game that would help teach writing skills.

Brainstorm with other people you trust and see what ideas you can come up with and then begin working to make those things happen. The more you do this, the more you will be able to make and the better you will get at satisfying the customers that come to you.

Step 17. Follow the Roadmap To Millions In Months

> *You're not going to make $2.5 million dollars very easily with a single book.*
>
> Turning PROBLEMS Into PROFITS

Turning Problems Into Profits

This is how you can take the solution you found to just one problem and build real profits with it by packaging it into multiple products that will help you go from your initial investment in this book to $2.5 million dollars in as little as 15 months. Sound incredible? Buckle up. This is going to be good.

START WITH A BOOK

You're not going to make $2.5 million dollars very easily with a single book. When you're self-publishing, the maximum you can expect to make is about $5 per book. You would need to sell 500,000 copies to make that money.

The reason you write the book is that it acts as the foundation of the other content you're going to create. Outlining the book gives you a roadmap that you can use to do other things and filling in the content helps you think through what you're going to present and how you will present it.

Your goal is to sell 100 copies of your book a month, or 3 copies a day. You might need to pay for some advertising to accomplish this, but if you've targeted your audience properly and you have been interacting with those Facebook groups and serving the organizations that support those people, you will have an easier time of it.

Selling 100 copies a month will net you $500. Not very impressive yet, but we're not done. You take that money and invest it in implementing the next step.

CREATE A MASTERCLASS

A $250 masterclass is affordable for most people but still signals high value and takes just one day of your time to host. You can break the chapters of your book into 30 minute segments of instruction and give yourself plenty of time to cover the content.

Put together no more than 10 minutes of instruction followed by 15 minutes of a fun activity and then 5 mintues for self-reflection.

Offer a tote bag with the paperback version of your book, a workbook, and a journal that you create to match the book as part of the incentive to sign up. You'll also want to put some advertising into the masterclass.

Figure that by the time you get done with materials, paying for space to host the class, and advertising, you'll be spending $50 per person. You end up making $200 per person. Run 4 Masterclasses a month and fill them with 25 people per class.

That will bring you in $20,000 per month, and $60,000 within that first quarter. You can run those every Saturday and use those live classes to get instant feedback about the best way to present

Turning Problems Into Profits

your roadmap and where your students are struggling so you can create the support materials that will help them overcome those challenges.

After that first quarter, you're ready for the next step. Set aside $10,000 from that $60,000 to invest in creating the recordings of your masterclass

RECORD YOUR MASTERCLASS

When you've run 12 of these masterclasses, you're ready for the next step. Record yourself doing one of your masterclasses. You're going to sell the recorded content for $250 and you're going to increase the fee for your live masterclass to $2,500 and include access to the recorded content plus the book as part of the value you add to your live masterclass.

You sell 25 people a day on your recorded class with a $200 profit, so you earn $5,000 a day which comes out to $150,000 a month or $1,800,000 in a year.

Your live courses are bringing in a profit of $2,000 per person and you're enrolling 100 people per month. You're making $200,000 a month on these live classes or $2,400,000 per year.

You're now making $350,000 per month off the recording and your live masterclass alone. You've made your $2.5 million by the end of month 15 and you're not even done making money yet.

DESIGN A GROUP COACHING PROGRAM

To increase the value of your offering, create a group coaching program around your content. Group coaching programs don't have to be complex to be effective. Hold a one hour training every week and every two weeks get your group coaching clients together for a hotseat session on the progress they are making with your coaching. Deliver the group coaching over a three-month time span and charge $25,000 per student per month to be in it.

Estimate your expenses at about $5000. Limit this to 12 students a quarter so you can create an intimate setting. You will be making $240,000 per month for this or $2,880,000 per year. From these group coaching students, you are going to recruit your one-on-one coaching clients.

OFFER A ONE-ON-ONE COACHING PROGRAM

Your time is now the single most valuable commodity that you have and you want to be selective in the amount of one-on-one clients you accept. One-on-one candidates should be paying you no less than $250,000 per month or $3 million dollars per year as you are going to be giving them the keys to the kingdom along with your help and support tapping into the success you've been experiencing.

FOLLOWING THE ROADMAP TO ABUNDANCE

What I've laid out in front of you is the absolute best-case scenario. It ignores your learning curve. Your results will probably take at least twice or even three times as long to achieve, depending on how far from being ready for success you are. I've given you a shortcut, but I can't give you the skills and the mindset you need to get there in one book. Nobody can.

Getting your mind right first is the most important work you can do to accelerate your success. A real estate investor I know who has experienced great success in the industry and built a multi-million dollar business as a result of it states in his book, A Millionaire's Treasure Map To Real Estate Investing Success, that there are 7 secrets to success in real estate investing or anything else you want to do in life. His 7 secrets are: get your mind right, seek wisdom, develop skills, make detailed plans, take massive action, form great alliances and be persistent.

I agree with what he says. There is nothing more important than getting your mind right and seeking wisdom. Spend at least an hour every day reading one of the books I recommend and gleaning from it the information you need to get your mind right.

I will add something to his 7 secrets: Learn to write. I don't care if you were good at it in school. You can become good at it by practicing. Learning to write is an exercise in creative problem solving. The better you become at writing, the better you will become at articulating your thoughts and communicating with others and the better you will also become at problem solving.

Develop these skills. Practice them every day. Be prepared to fail but don't quit and don't give up. If you persist in putting the things I've discussed into practice and you follow the roadmap I've given you, you can succeed on levels you've never succeeded before. You have it in you to do so.

LET S TALK OPTIONS

If you're an individual, business owner, or CEO who is interested in discovering what I can do to help you or your business get on the path to turning your problems into profits, email me at brandy@40daywriter.com. The initial consultation is free.

Step 18. Prepare For Success

> *My problem in success was NOT what I had or did not have. It was the measuring stick that I was using to gauge whether or not I was a success.*
>
> Turning PROBLEMS Into PRO*fits*BLEMS

I did not plan, originally, to include this chapter but upon reflection I would be remiss if I did not include it. I would be doing a disservice both to you and to the people you serve.

When you begin a business, you are stepping into a role of leadership. It's going to change your whole life because it's going to change the way you look at and think about your life. I want to help you prepare yourself for success by setting the stage for what to expect and to guide you in navigating the challenges that will come your way.

DEFINE SUCCESS BEFORE YOU SEEK IT

I was 32 years old and absolutely miserable. I was nearly in tears as I sat down at my work station. I felt like a total failure in life because I didn't have a car, I didn't have a house, my bank account was in the negatives, I owed more than I made, I didn't have a title, I didn't have a degree, and I was not – by any of the standards that our society uses to measure it – a success. I was comparing myself to other people who had not traveled the road I'd been on and seeing myself falling short of their achievements.

I sent up a prayer to God and I asked for His help in seeing myself through his eyes. I didn't know what to expect. I flipped open the Bible, looking for some words of encouragement in there and my eyes fell upon the passage in Luke where Jesus stated, "Foxes have dens and birds of the sky have nests, but the son of Man has nowhere to rest his head."

At the time I worked in the marketing department for a major Fortune 500 company. We spent over 2 billion dollars a year on marketing alone. We considered ourselves a success if our marketing attempts reached even 1/10th of the people we were trying to reach. We also knew that the day we stopped our marketing is the day our business would stop growing.

I had to ask myself, in that moment, did I consider Jesus a failure? Here's is a man who, essentially, took a small mom-and-pop business and turned it into the single most successful multi-level marketing venture the world has ever seen. And he did that on a $0 marketing budget.

Furthermore, his success didn't end with him. It didn't really start until after his death. He managed to go from 12 disciples in a backwater portion of the Roman Empire to having not one single continent where His name has not been spoken. His teachings can be found in every language. His message continues to spread even when there is no official leadership to spread it.

There are still people today singing his jingles, buying his programs, and striving to gain access to the things he taught in his three short years of ministry. From a marketing standpoint, the man was the most successful marketer in the history of the world.

Yet he had none – not even one – of the trappings of success that our society uses to measure such things. He was not a degreed person. The Pharisees flat out asked him what his credentials were for teaching, because He didn't have any.

He was not rich. He didn't own a house. He relied on the kindness of strangers. He didn't own a horse – the equivalent of a vehicle back in those days. He borrowed the ass on which he rode into Jerusalem. He had no job and no fancy title. Yet people gave him money purely for the value he brought to their lives.

My problem in success was NOT what I had or did not have. It was the measuring stick that I was using to gauge whether or not I was a success. I was using the wrong measuring stick.

I asked myself, "What did Jesus use as His measuring stick?"

As I studied scripture, the answer came to me: relationships. He measured His success by the quality and the quantity of the relationships that He developed with the people around Him. That was His secret, and I determined to make it my secret, too. It was in studying the life of Christ and what He did that I uncovered the truth about what leadership is.

LEARN TO LEAD

I didn't realize it when I first started trying to build a business, but entrepreneurship is a leadership position. You may not be aware of that fact, either, but it is true. You are leading people on a life-changing journey from where they are to where they want to be, and that is a big responsibility.

Many people believe that leadership is telling other people what to do. That's not leadership. That's being bossy. Here is how I spell leadership:

Love. This is not mushy, feeling-based love. It is the kind of love that is always acting for the good of the other person even when that requires great sacrifice on your own part. If your business isn't founded in that kind of love, you can force your success but it'll be like pushing a car uphill. Every step will be painful and difficult.

Empathy. This is why I spent so much time talking about listening to understand and trying to see the world through their eyes. If you can't see it through their eyes, you won't be able to translate what you want them to do into words that they can understand.

Turning Problems Into Profits

Accountability. You need to hold yourself accountable for the results you produce, and that means you need to listen to critics. They may be way off base, but they will be the best at helping you find and fix your faults if you allow them to be.

You will hear many success gurus tell you to cut the negative people out of your life because they're just obstacles in your path. I am going to tell you the truth: I have gained more wisdom and more insight from the negative people who were in my life than I have from all of the positive people who cheered me on and gave me words of encouragement. Just as a car battery works only when it has a negative charge and a positive charge, so too will you find your business to be far better when you have both kinds of people in your life.

No blaming other people or your circumstances when things go wrong. Take ownership of the problems and the mistakes you make. Work to fix them. Blame is an easy escape from responsibility, but it handicaps you and prevents you from looking for ways that you can stop the problem from happening.

Discipleship. Good leaders are always mindful that someday, they won't be there to share their gifts with others and help push their visions forward. Because of that, they invest the time and energy in identifying potential leaders in the people that follow them and then cultivating those people to be the next generation of leaders. They teach them the skills and the mindset needed so the next generation doesn't miss out because the leader wasn't there to pass it on.

Encouragement. Discouragement is going to come when you set out to do anything new in life. It's part of the process of testing you and shaping you into the person you must become to claim your success. It's not meant to get you to quit or give up. It's meant to get you asking yourself why you are doing what you are doing and why doing that is worth the price you're paying.

Once you find your why, a why so big it makes you cry when you think about it, you'll find the wings that will help you fly past the obstacles in your way. You need to become very good at spotting when discouragement is taking root in the hearts of the people who are following you and then finding the words to say to give them the hope they need to rekindle their commitment to the vision and move forward.

Relationships. Investing the time to get to know the people who follow you on a deep and personal level is critical to earning and retaining their loyalty. Remembering their names, their personal preferences, their hopes and dreams, makes them feel like they matter to you and it will inspire in them loyalty to you.

Turning Problems Into Profits

You also want to work to connect the people that follow you together and encourage them to develop relationships with one another. The stronger the bonds between you and your followers, and between your followers themselves, the more likely they are to keep working together even when you aren't there to oversee it.

Service. Many people are used to the model of reigning from on high, giving orders to those beneath you. This kind of leadership, though, is exhausting. It doesn't inspire loyalty and so you're constantly having to oversee the people beneath you to be sure the work is getting done.

If you look at leadership as you working to serve the people who follow you so that they in turn can serve others, you will have less stress and more loyalty. You will get more done with less effort. They will trust that when you give them orders, it's only for their benefit which means you are less likely to meet resistance when you do give those orders.

Humility. Humor and humility both come from the same root word. The ability to laugh at yourself and your own mistakes will ease tension and make it easier for the people beneath you to handle their own failures.

Humility is also about recognizing and honoring the contributions of other people to your success. Nobody – and I do mean nobody – succeeds alone. You wouldn't be here without the contributions of not only your parents but every ancestor that came before your parents.

Acknowledging and honoring those contributions will encourage people to be more likely to be generous with the time and talent and energy the invest in you because they are confident you will recognize and appreciate the work that they've done on your behalf.

Integrity. Integrity means doing your best not to ask of anyone else what you wouldn't personally be willing to do. You don't recommend things unless you have personally tried them and know them to be beneficial to others.

You do your best to live your life aligned with the beliefs you hold. What comes out of your mouth should always reflect those beliefs and the actions you take should be an extension of those beliefs.

When you live with integrity, not only do you have less worries about feeling imposter syndrome, other people know what to expect from you and that begins to create confidence in what you say and do, which builds trust.

Purpose. Have a bigger purpose in mind than just making money. Envision all the lives you are going to impact and what that will do for those lives if you succeed. Now, imagine the impact that helping these people will have on the lives of those who love them.

How will the community improve if those individuals and families are helped? How will this change the region in which you live if more communities like yours are getting this help and support? How will the country change? How will the world at large change – all because you lived out your purpose?

In all things you do and say, devote yourself to this purpose. Always ask yourself whether what you are about to do or say is going to bring you closer to that purpose or take you further away from it. Live by it. Write it on your heart.

When people know that you are never going to ask them to do anything and that you are never going to say anything that is out of alignment with that purpose, they are more likely to jump on board with you because they know where that purpose will take them if they do.

THE PHASES OF SUCCESS

You are looking to help people solve their problems, and you would expect that doing so will make their lives better right away, but how quickly your solution improves their lives will depend a great deal on where they are starting in life. You want to be prepared to coach people through the phases of success so they don't get scared off and quit too soon to get the benefits.

The Destruction Phase

When you start out to do any great thing, you can expect your life to turn upside down. People you thought would support you won't and may even actively discourage you. The things you thought would come together won't. You may lose friends, family, or things that you value.

Most people take this as a sign to quit, give up, and go do something else. However, it's important to understand what is happening here so that you don't make that same mistake.

Imagine that you are a real estate investor who has bought a piece of land with incredible potential. However, it's currently covered in rubble and debris. It's got a cracked and bubbled foundation from the last owner who was too impatient to build correctly. Everything on it needs to go before you can begin to build.

You bring in a bulldozer and you start destroying. You start ripping up that foundation and you start hauling out that rubble. You have to. If you were to build on top of it, nothing you built would be stable or would last long.

That piece of land with incredible potential is

you. The developer that bought the land is God. God is going to start destroying everything in your life, not to hurt you, but to remove from your life everything that would stand in the way of you achieving your greatest possible good.

The harder you cling to what's being destroyed in your life, the longer this process will take and the worse the pain will be. It's important to recognize what is happening so you don't cling to the old and can release and allow the new to be built in your life. Once that destruction phase is over, there will be a new period of time in your life: construction.

The Construction Phase

This is a period where things are better, but still not good. You can catch glimpses of the future that awaits you as the framework of the building goes up, but you can't yet take residence in it.

You will feel frustration as you get impatient and eager for the construction to finally be finished so you can take residence in this dream.

You will feel discouragement as you wonder if it will ever be done. You will be tempted to give up and walk away. If you do, you will miss out on the greater things to come. Instead, this is the time to refocus on reminding yourself why this journey matters. Why does it matter that you succeed in changing other people's lives? Why does it matter that you help other people solve their problems? Why is it worth all the pain you're going to go through to get there?

Construction is messy. Noisy. Always busy. Sometimes you're going to feel overwhelmed with the amount of activity going on and the amount of mess that accumulates in your life. During these moments, step back from the scene and trust that the timing for all that's being done will be perfect.

The Occupation and Maintenance Phase

One day, just when you thought it least likely to happen, you're going to look and find the construction is complete. The dream is realized, and you can finally take ownership and move in.

However, even in this phase, nothing is going to be perfect. You'll still need to decorate and tidy up and furnish that dream to reflect your tastes. You're going to need to maintain the dream and feed it everything it needs to stay healthy and continue growing.

The Expansion and Improvement Phase

You will need to continue expanding and improving yourself if you want to keep your business growing and thriving. Your business is built on the foundation of your personal growth, and like any foundation, cracks will develop, and things will start to collapse if you try to put more weight on that foundation than it was built to handle. Read books, seek mentors, take classes, and always, always, always seek to learn and grow and improve yourself.

SUPPORT IS IMPORTANT

This is a journey that is best taken with other people who are ready and willing to support you in getting where you want to go. If you're looking for that kind of help and support, start by joining the Professional Problem Solvers Network, our free Facebook group.

Step 19. Join the Human Development Investment Group

> There are plenty of under-developed human beings out there waiting for people to invest in them and, like empty or run-down houses, with the right help and support they can be renovated and put back to work for the benefit of their communities.
>
> Turning PROBLEMS Into PRO*its*BLEMS

Turning Problems Into Profits

It isn't fair and it isn't right, but you will end up paying about 40% of the money you earn from the services you provide to the IRS. That is - unless you take that money and invest it. Investments are taxed and treated very differently from earned income. This is one way the rich stay rich. They invest their money

Investments allow you to multiply your money without multiplying the amount of work you do. You earn a percentage of other people's earned income in return for the investment you made. All while saving yourself a lot of money.

WHAT MAKES REAL ESTATE INVESTING WORTH DOING

Many people turn to real estate investing as a way of putting their money to work for them. I have a Real Estate Investor that I know by the name of Dennis Henson. He has been in that business for more than 40 years. He refers to Real Estate Investing as the Royal Flush of Investing.

If you don't play poker, a Royal Flush is the one hand you can hold that virtually guarantees a win for you. There is no hand that's better. Unless someone else – by some miracle – also happens to hold a Royal Flush, you're going to get the whole pot at the end of that game.

The reasons that he considers Real Estate to be a

Royal Flush is that it checks off all five of the investing check boxes:

- Leverage
- Inflation
- Revenue Production
- Tax Advantages
- The Power of Compound Interest

Leverage: You can hold a $100,000 property for as little as $10,000.

Inflation: Real Estate property values experience exponential growth. For example, the median property value in 1940 was $2,000. By 1970, it was up to $23,000. By 2007, it was over $150,000. There are very few other things you can invest in that will give you that keep pace with the rate of inflation that same way.

Revenue Production: You don't have to have a property paid off for it to profit you. You remember that $100,000 property you bought for $10,000 with leverage? Let's say you rent that out. Your mortgage is $500 a month.

You pay $200 for insurance and $100 for property taxes and you set aside $200 for repair costs. You charge your renter $1500 a month and you pocket the extra $500. You pay $0 for the house and you make $500 a month for owning it.

Tax Advantages: There are a ton of tax benefits to owning a home. You can deduct most of your expenses and property depreciation, plus there are deductions for taxes paid and even for interest paid on your mortgage.

Those tax deductions means that the money you pay out for repairs, property taxes, and insurance on the house gets paid for up front by the renter and then you get an extra $500 paid to you by the government on top of that as reimbursement. That's powerful.

Compound Interest: When you lend money to someone to buy your house, you can charge them compound interest. That compound interest ads up quickly even when it's at a low rate. You are earning money every single day that loan is out there and you aren't doing anything extra to get that money.

There are some other advantages to Real Estate Investing, too:

1) Real Estate isn't going anywhere and is less likely to be lost overnight than virtually any other investment you can make;

2) You can control all the decisions made about the investment meaning you can control the outcome much easier than with other investments like stocks or bonds.

3) Cities love Real Estate Investors because they take problem properties that are empty or run down and renovate them and get tax-paying property owners back in them.

However, there are known problems with real estate investing.

THE KNOWN PROBLEMS WITH REAL ESTATE INVESTING

Real estate Investing is neither fool proof nor easy to do. Another investor I know, Roger D. Paschal, calls himself the Miracle Investor. He told me the reason he called himself that is because if your real estate venture makes a profit, it's a miracle. And he's very good at making profits on his Real Estate ventures.

However, the ordinary person does not have his years of experience or insider knowledge that helps him to know exactly which properties to pick and which are better left alone. The ordinary investor, therefore, is going to end up taking a bath on most of the investments they make while they learn the ropes.

Turning Problems Into Profits

Furthermore, Real Estate Investment is heavily dependent upon the market. If there's a crash or a bubble burst, your Real Estate Investment could go from being worth millions to being worth thousands overnight. Yes, the market will readjust itself eventually, but the gamble is whether it will readjust itself in time for you to avoid going under.

Additionally, there's so much competition for Real Estate because, let's face it, new Real Estate does not get made every day. Earthquakes, mudslides, tornadoes, and hurricanes are all threats to your investment, but it's rare to have whole square acres of land suddenly pop up overnight for you to invest your money in developing.

Even if it did, it would take some time before it was something that other people might want to buy. It's not going to pop up with a house planted on it, roads to get to it, connected to electricity and internet capable. That's going to take your money to develop.

Another problem brought about by the trend of investing in real estate without also investing in helping the lower income populations achieve financial independence is a sharp uptick of homeless individuals. The fierce competition for the limited number of parcels of land available to buy in developed cities leads people buy up troubled properties and rehabilitate them, charging 3-5 times what they were worth in rent.

The people who were once residents of that property can no longer afford to live there and the amount of housing they can afford decreases by the day.

It's happening in all the major cities all around the world. It's causing a huge crisis in terms of the spreading of disease and debris, and it's also resulting in a major real estate bubble where there are more properties on the market than there are people who can afford to rent or buy them.

The last and final problem with real estate investing is finding good renters and maintaining the property. Renters, because they have no stake in the property, don't have an incentive to care about fixing the place up or increasing its value. If they don't know how to turn their problems into profits, they can get laid off or fired and end up missing payments. Your profitable property can quickly become a financial nightmare.

Yes, you can evict, but that process is lengthy and expensive. It can take you a while to find a new tenant. If you sell it, you have to find a buyer and close a deal. There are all kinds of challenges to be had with real estate investing.

STOCKS

Another place that comes highly recommended for investing is stocks.

Turning Problems Into Profits

Benefits of Buying Stocks

Buying stock allows you to take advantage of the lower tax rates offered to investors while insulating yourself from the stress and insecurities of personally running and owning a business. You get a vote in what happens, but you don't have to get personally involved in doing the work.

It's like betting on the person that runs the company and the product or service they produce. When you win, you can win big. People who bought Microsoft stock when it was first released to the public paid $21 per share. That same stock is now worth $137 per share. When the company profits, so do you.

Some companies pay monthly dividends, so if you have the right combination of stocks and the right amount of it, you can literally collect a check every week from these companies without having to do any work at all to make that money. The amount of money you make from them is solely based on the amount of money you've invested in them and that's it.

Disadvantages of Stock

Just like with real estate, you have to know what you are doing in order to make profits with stocks. They are even more vulnerable because their value rests entirely on the decision-making capability of the heads of the companies and organizations that issue the stocks or the bonds. That means there's very little way for you to control the outcome of your investment. You get one vote per share, but when there may be a thousand shares or more, that vote may not count for much.

Furthermore, the value of the stock depends heavily on the opinions of the people who hold that stock. Panicky people can undervalue a stock in a hurry by selling so much of it that it can go from being worth a thousand dollars or more a share to being worth pennies on the dollar in just a day. My grandfather was worth millions until the stock market crash of 2001. In a single day, his net worth went from millions to a few hundred thousand. He didn't live to see the market recover.

Also, stocks have limitations on the value they can bring to you. You're slicing up just one pie, and the more slices that you create, the less of a percentage of that pie that you get. The pie will hopefully grow, and that's one of the ways you increase the amount of money you get out of your investment, but your percentage of it won't grow with it unless you buy more stocks or there's a stock split which means you get more slices but each slice is worth less.

Last, there's no emotional return on investment with a stock or bond purchase. You are disconnected from the people that the companies you invest in serve and you don't usually get to see firsthand the benefits that your investment brings to the lives of others.

A BETTER WAY TO INVEST: THE HUMAN DEVELOPMENT INVESTMENT GROUP (H-DIG)

The best way to invest is to combine the advantages of stocks with the benefits of real estate investing. How? Through the Human Development Investment Group.

There are plenty of underdeveloped human beings out there waiting for people to invest in them and, like empty or run-down houses, with the right help and support they can be renovated and put back to work for the benefit of the communities in which they reside.

These people have a virtually unlimited supply of problems they know how to solve that can benefit everyone, but they don't know what they've got and they lack the connections they need to help them find it, mine it, refine it, package and present it. That's where H-DIG would step in to lend their support.

Leverage: Imagine if you could take $50,000 and leverage it to hold onto an investment that was worth BILLIONS of dollars. That's the power of the Human Development Investment group. One investment of $50,000 in a single underdeveloped human being can produce a steady stream of solutions that can be packaged and sold, representing billions of dollars in untapped value.

Inflation: Your ability to increase the value of your investment isn't dependent upon inflation. Every problem that on underdeveloped person knows how to solve is a new potential revenue stream to be tapped into which can exponentially multiply the value of your investment.

Revenue Production: The $50,000 you pledge begins getting paid back within 90 days of the initial investment at a rate of 25% of the profits until the full amount – with interest – is paid back and then 5% in perpetuity.

Tax Advantages: The H-DIG would be operated as an S-Corp so you would be receiving dividends from stock instead of earned income. You get the advantages of stock investing but since you pick the person you are choosing to invest in and you choose the problems you want to support them in solving, you have direct control over where your money goes and you get direct input on the decisions made about that business.

Compound Profits: Rather than charging a compound interest rate to increase your earnings, you are compounding your profits by assisting each underdeveloped human being cultivate and develop multiple streams of income – each of which profits you. Since you receive a small percentage

Turning Problems Into Profits

of that profit for life, your profits grow as theirs do.

Tax Benefits: To decrease the stress and increase the likelihood of success for each person that H-Dig adopts to help, we will invest in purchasing a distressed HUD or foreclosure property for that person and their family, then provide them a rent-to-own contract. The community achieves dual benefits of real estate properties that are rehabilitated and restored along with a person who might have formerly been a drain on the system now becoming a contributing, productive member of it. H-Dig gets all the tax benefits of property ownership while virtually guaranteeing itself a stable renter who will care for the property as if it were their own – because some day, it will be.

Investing in small businesses is usually considered a high-risk proposition because most small business owners don't know sound business principles before they begin. They are usually investing in high expense items like inventory or retail space, and they are focused on putting their money into websites and logos that actually don't need to be created until later down the road.

This system minimizes those risks. We are starting with a tested product – a problem they know how to solve – and using their experience to find the right target market. We are then selling to an established audience.

Brandy M. Miller

Imagine if you'd been able to invest just a little of your money into Apple or Microsoft or Facebook when it came out. How wealthy would you be right now?

Intrigued? FInd out more by emailing brandy@40daywriter.com subject H-DIG.

Case Studies

> These businesses all began with a problem that need solving — your business can, too.
>
> Turning PROBLEMS Into PRO*fits*BLEMS

Turning Problems Into Profits

There are three ways you can test any premise. The first is by doing things that are suggested to you, but this might lead to disaster. The second is by not doing things that are suggested to you, but that also might lead to disaster. The best way is to study what others have done with the advice being given and see where it led people.

The businesses on these next pages all began with a problem that needed to be solved. These women turned their problems into profits, and you can, too.

CASE STUDY 1: LATAUSHA TAYLOR

LaTausha Taylor is a 41-year-old mother of three and a former recording artist. "I'm still a songwriter. I was once a recording artist. I've also owned a record label and a music publishing company."

She was originally from Indianapolis, Indiana before relocating to Mobile, Alabama and then moving on to Fayetteville once her children were grown and gone. "I came to visit a good friend of mine that moved to Fayetteville and in two weeks I had an apartment and a job. I said to myself, I guess this is my new home."

The independence and freedom of the empty nest is still new. "I was a teenage mom so I've had my kids to raise the majority of my life. I kind of feel guilty that I'm so excited about this new world."

Brandy M. Miller

She now acts a brand consultant for independent musicians and corporate brands when she isn't working at her full-time position at a non-profit organization in her current hometown of Fayetteville, North Carolina called Action Pathways, Inc.

"They (Action Pathways) are a nonprofit anti-poverty organization here in Fayetteville. I love the work that we do every day. Every program we have is tailored toward helping the community, individuals, and families become economically and socially sound, ensuring their total wellbeing. We house the Second Harvest Food Bank. We oversee the Head Start program. We have a reentry program that helps ex-felons once they come out of a correctional institution. There is an Aspire Program up under the umbrella for self-sufficiency, job training and life skills development. They offer a home weatherization program as well. Again, they have everything to help the community and those that are less fortunate. So it is rewarding work we do every day."

She loves the work she does, but it's definitely not her dream job. "I'm wide awake and definitely not dreaming when I go in there. I think my dream job is to just be a help to others that want to help themselves. While it's not necessarily my dream job, it does compliment who I am and my personality in terms of helping the world."

Her passion is in the music and entertainment industry. If money was not an issue, I would be helping the millions and millions of artists in the world that don't have the knowledge of the music business, how to brand themselves, how to market themselves, and, in most cases, don't have the budget. I would be able to be more of an investor with my clients as well. So that would be my dream job. Just travel the world, tour with them, do the nightlife events, and just have fun... while making money."

Her heart for musicians, entertainers and emerging brands is such that, while she's making money doing it, she's certainly not getting rich. "I've done a lot of gratuitous service that should have been business and paid jobs, but I think that ultimately if you're able to help clients understand how to position themselves, and give them some fuel for their fire, it can change things for them. I teach the people I work with that it's a hobby, hustle, & business and in that order. As artists and entrepreneurs, we're going to do this anyway. We love to write, we love to perform, and do all these different things. That's the hobby. If you don't lose the love for it, it'll never seem like work, but also you have to know that it's a billion-dollar business. I help them get from hobby to business.

Working with her entertainers and musicians serves an additional purpose, too. "It keeps me connected to the industry. I'm still connected to that part of the business and able to continue to keep my pulse on new trends"

The biggest challenge she faces in pursuing her dream career of being a highly sought after brand consultant/manager is social media and marketing. It's not my strength and sometimes I neglect that very important part of building the business.

"Originally, one of my biggest challenges was my location. Again, I'm originally from Indianapolis, but there's no large music presence there. There are no record labels or publishing agents or anything like that in Indianapolis. Then, when I moved down south to Mobile, Alabama, just imagine there being even less of an industry presence. So, until now, all of my frustrations and challenges have come from my location, even though we have this big world with social media and things of that nature, that's another challenge for me. Although I know exactly what I want to do and how to do it and how to meet my clients' needs, I have a hit and miss love affair with social media. Some days I'm hot, other days I'm like, does it require all of this? And then I sit back and think, man, if I had somebody to run my social media and help with my marketing, I could be the best brand consultant this industry has ever seen."

However, LaTausha isn't just wishing on a star to fix those challenges. "I'm in Fayetteville now, so I'm five hours from Atlanta, seven hours from New York, and able to travel to those locations and network and be a part of the thriving industry there. I'm also taking the time out to work with established social media managers that can help build my business and followers to generate more clientele and affiliates to work with.

LaTausha is what she calls an #entrepremogul - somebody who knows they want to be an entrepreneur and has the characteristics of an entrepreneur, but isn't quite sure which one of those entrepreneurial ventures is going to be their sweet spot or be the big boom. As a result, they often take on multiple ventures. In fact, she's been involved in a number of business ventures over the years. "Part of my journey to be an entrepreneur. I've done MCA, Prepaid Legal, Noni juice, you know, you name it. I've tried it. I've also owned a beauty salon and nail parlor although I don't personally provide any of the services. The ultimate goal is to diversify and create multiple streams of revenue.

After encountering multiple clients with great ideas and/or strategies to reach their goals but NO BUDGET to execute, she knew she had to find other ways to be compensated. Over the past year, she was introduced to Business Credit, Gold, and Cryptocurrency. She learned how to generate revenue using alternatives to Cash and Personal Credit.

It significantly changed the way she serviced

Brandy M. Miller

her clients and generated additional streams of income. Those interested in learning more about how to establish Business Credit, Save Gold in small denominations and/or acquire Cryptocurrency can email her at IamLatausha@gmail.com to get more information.

Turning Problems Into Profits

CASE STUDY 2: BRITTANY WASHINGTON

Brittany Washington is the founder of My Beautiful Fluff, a fashion company focused on providing body positive clothing to women who are in the plus-sized range. Although she envisions a future of boutique stores and other types of clothing, her company is currently based around t-shirts.

The company is a dream in the making, but started out as a happy accident. "I always wanted a plus sized boutique. The t-shirts were a happy accident. I went natural and I wanted a cute little natural hair t-shirt that had all the little jewels and all that stuff on it, but I couldn't find them in my size.

I was like, "This stinks." My choices were either to buy two t-shirts and sew them together or to keep looking for what I needed. I eventually found one in a 4x, but it was super expensive. It was also definitely a man's shirt just with a female design on it. I had to cut the sleeves, cut a neck, and it was just a mess. That made me think, "There's gotta be something out there. I know there's more people that have natural hair that are a little on the fluffier side besides me."

It's the details that designers miss when they are trying to scale clothing designed for smaller women to fit larger women which Brittany intends to focus on delivering.

"I made sure that there's more width in the arms because I hate putting on a shirt and feeling like the incredible hulk, where the seams are pulling, and I can't feel my arms at the top because it's that tight."

She intends to go head-to-head with major brands who are just now putting together sizes for the larger woman.

"We need more stuff for fluffy figures. It's nice to be included in some of these other brands, but I don't want to be just an afterthought. I don't want to deal with brands that are looking and saying, 'Okay, it's popular, so let me make something for bigger sizes right now because it's the in thing to do'. If you've been in business five, ten years and you have just started plus sizes in the last one, two, or three years, I don't want it. I don't want your perfume, your lip gloss, or anything else."

One of the biggest challenges she's faced in building her business so far has been working with overseas manufacturers.

"It gets easier with practice, but it's definitely not for the faint at heart."

Getting over the language barrier and getting the sizing right are the main obstacles to working with overseas manufacturers.

Turning Problems Into Profits

"The first box of tee shirts that I got when ordering from overseas were supposed to be white t-shirts with a colorful design, sized large through 4x, equal sizes of each one. I got one box of green t-shirts, all in 4x. Plus, instead of inches, the sizes were all in centimeters so they were smaller than expected. I was like, 'Oh, my God. Am I going to cry, or do I call them and go off? I don't know what to do!"

However, Brittany persevered. She envisions making My Beautiful Fluff a household name, with subscription boxes and a retail boutique in her current location of Davenport, Iowa so that women can come and try things on in person.

My Beautiful Fluff was not Brittany's first venture into entrepreneurship. She tried several different MLM companies and several different investment opportunities before her company began experiencing success. Like many people, she invested in a 401(k) while she was working a 9-5 position and got involved with several different MLM companies as she worked to build a future for herself and her family.

"It's a quick place to learn and if you're at the top it's great, but even if you recruit 100 people with some of them, you still really aren't making anything."

Those early business failures caused her to lose some friends along the way, and it made her remaining friends and family more skeptical of every new venture she tried.

"They don't see the growth you've gone through or the work you've done to improve yourself since the last time you failed. All they see is, "Oh? Yeah? You're on your sixth one now. If 1-5 didn't work, why is this one different? They won't even tell you nicely at this point. They'll just say, 'This is stupid. Why do you keep giving your money out?'" They'll also ask you, '"What is this one now? How many weeks is it going to be before you're done with this one?'."

She didn't let those words discourage her, though. She continued searching for her opportunity to succeed, something she is definitely finding with My Beautiful Fluff.

"I've partnered and done some events, including some fashion shows and some community events."

The fashion show was very successful. "It was a learning experience. I was nervous, but it went really well. The models were amazing. The event was good, and the crowd was enthusiastic. It was just a good experience."

Her plan is to branch out and do her own fashion show next year. She also wants to test an affiliate program with her current brand ambassadors to see how it goes.

"I want to just kind of work out all the kinks. I don't want to put it out and then say, 'Let's work through the kinks' after I've signed a bunch of people. No. Let's start with the four or five. We'll see how it works, what we can tweak, and learn and grow from there before we launch it out to everybody."

Her problem became her profit. You can find out more about Brittany and My Beautiful Fluff by visiting mybeautifulfluff.com

CASE STUDY 3: AIMMEE KODACHIAN

Aimmee Kodachian was born with dyslexia and dreamed of being a teacher. However, when the Lebanese civil war of 1975 broke out, a bomb literally dropped into the middle of her life. That bomb killed her oldest brother and sent her family flying in all directions. She was forced to drop out of school with only a fourth-grade education.

She faced numerous obstacles, but it was in the middle of that darkness that she tapped into an unexpected source of help she calls The Negotiator Mind. It was this still, calm voice that spoke to her in the worst moment of her life and guided her forward on a path to achieving more than she'd ever dreamed possible, one which would eventually lead her to turning her problems into profits.

It was the Negotiator Mind that led her to America with her 9-year-old daughter. Unable to read, write, or speak English, many thought she should just give up and turn back, but Aimmee persevered and relied on her Negotiator Mind to lead her forward.

Eventually, she would write a book, Tears of Hope, and become a key note speaker. She found a new way to teach and to pass on her wisdom, one that made her money and didn't require a degree to do it.

Turning Problems Into Profits

Today, Aimmee is the Special Liaison Office for the Women's Federation for World Peace, International. She is the producer of the Empowering Humanity TV show and founder of The Negotiator Mind program.

Her goal is to reach as many people as possible and to teach them how to step into their light, reach their dreams, and to empower humanity to do great things no matter where they begin life.

You can learn more about Aimmee and her story by visiting her websites: NegotiatorMind.com and EmpoweringHumanity.com.

CASE STUDY 4: THE AND I THOUGHT LADIES

When you dream of being a best-selling author, but you don't have the network connections to pull it off and you have trouble getting interviewed by the people in all the right places, what do you do?

If you're Wilnona Marie and Jade Dee of the And I Thought Ladies fame, you create your own opportunities. When I first met them in 2016, it was on a podcast run by a lady in Great Britain named Segilola Salami. Jade Dee and Wilnona Marie were her guests, and I was on with them. We were discussing my vision for creating a 40 Day Writer Reality TV show where 40 writers would compete over 40 days to finish, polish, and pitch their books to publishers who would then compete for the rights to publish those works.

At the time, I'd assembled a crew of coaches who were willing to help me train those writers in the business skills they would need to succeed, but I lacked the publishers and the financial backing to get the project going. That's why I was on the show, to spread the word and prepare for my launch.

From that show, Jade and Wilnona became some of my closest friends and staunchest supporters. They are the masters of creating oppor-

Turning Problems Into Profits

tunities. When told by a Hollywood producer that my idea was too "esoteric" to be successful despite the fact that while only 60% of the American population believes they could be entrepreneurs Shark Tank, a show about entrepreneurs pitching their business ideas to wealthy investors, has remained a hit show for nearly 10 seasons now. 80-90% of Americans believe they have a book in them. Jade and Wilnona decided to put her theory to the test and created a TV show entitled Just Writin' Life that aired on Amazon for several seasons.

They have created two magazines The And I Thought Literary Magazine and The 25 Hottest Indie Creatives Magazine. These magazines not only help them promote their own books but provide them leverage they need to get more network connections and interviews. They turned their problem of not getting enough publicity into not one but three profitable solutions that have helped them take giant steps closer to their dreams.

Because of their moxie and their persistence, they have walked the red carpets of Hollywood, rubbed shoulders with directors, producers, and actors, and have an army of successful authors, publishers, and agents they can call on to help them with any given project.

They have also become hosts of the Thoughtful

Brandy M. Miller

Book Awards show each year and an annual Las Vegas Experienced Writers Retreat.

You can learn more about Jade Dee and Wilnona Marie at http://www.andwethought.com/

Turning Problems Into Profits

CASE STUDY 5: LISA JONES

Lisa Jones was something of a daredevil as a child. At age 8, that daring nature resulted in a terrible bicycle accident where most of the skin was scraped off of her face. While the skin healed, she had continuous skin problems that weren't being helped by typical facial remedies available in the store.

She began experimenting with mixing together different lotions and ingredients from the kitchen, trying to come up with something that would help cure the blackheads and other problems she experienced. Recipe after recipe failed, but she kept trying.

Then her youngest daughter came home with a rash she couldn't get rid of and her oldest daughter suffered with eczema so bad she was ashamed to leave the house. Lisa knew she needed help – fast. She sent up a quick prayer to ask for God's guidance in developing a formula and – for the first time – found something that worked. The skin conditions were clearing up quickly and weren't coming back.

She wasn't interested in starting a business, but her family pushed her to start selling the product. Her husband wasn't initially supportive. He wasn't against it. He just didn't think she could compete in such a crowded marketplace.

That is, until she developed an after-shave to help him with rashes he developed after shaving that none of the regular brands could help. His problems went away, and so did his skepticism about her business idea. As a pharmacist, he was able to suggest ingredients she hadn't considered and steer her away from ingredients that were non-natural.

Every addition to her line has come as a direct result of helping someone else solve their skin-care problems. Her current line includes skin moisturizers and astringents for cleansing.

You can find Cura Bello products online at: https://www.curabelloskincare.com/

Turning Problems Into Profits

CASE STUDY 6: CLARA RUFAI

Clara Rufai had a serious problem. She was stuck in a job that she didn't feel fulfilled her purpose or gave her an opportunity to shine as brightly as she knew was possible for her. She wanted a business of her own, but her funds and time were tied up so tightly it seemed an impossibility.

She met a coach, Ava Eagle Brown, who suggested that she turn that problem – one shared by many hundreds of thousands of people the world over – into her first profitable venture and write a book. Clara took her advice and launched Prison Break: The 9 to 5 Escape Agenda: Taking the Leap from Limitation to Liberation in September of 2016.

She organized her first virtual Leap and Shine Conference in November of 2016, bringing in a team of entrepreneurship experts to help give advice and offer strategies for other aspiring "escapees." She continued building her brand through Facebook lives and YouTube releases over social media while developing her network connections.

Today, she is making powerful moves as a Shine Strategist, helping women the world over find their place to shine and take the steps they need to demonstrate their brilliance. Her first live Leap and Shine Conference is being held February 21-22nd, 2020 in London. Speakers from all over the world will be gathering to help train the men and women who attend that conference in the things they need to know to take their place among the stars and shine for all the world to see.

You can find out more about her Leap and Shine conference by visiting the website: https://www.leapandshineconference.com/

Her courage in stepping forward and sharing her story has led to her being featured on the cover of magazines, in radio and television interviews, and connecting with some of the most brilliant minds of today.

Learn more about Clara by visiting her website: https://www.clararufai.com/

Turning Problems Into Profits

CASE STUDY 7: JULI ROLAND

Juli Roland began her career as a custom matcher and consultant for a major paint company. She learned to match color by eye before the advent of computer color-scanning tools.

Seven years of hands-on experience in the paint world provided her with a solid understanding of pigments and coatings. Later, she further expanded her knowledge through the study of color science with famed strategist, Lori Sawaya.

She noticed a consistent problem among homeowners and commercial property owners alike: They weren't sure how to pick the right colors for their rehabilitations, remodeling, and renovation projects.

She took her knowledge and experience and developed a successful business helping property and homeowners increase the value of their properties using scientific paint-matching techniques to out the perfect paint colors for remodeling and renovations projects.

Today, she brings her expertise to projects and properties all over the DFW metroplex. You can find out more by visiting her website at http://paintcolorhelp.com

Recommended Reading

The Greatest Salesman in the World by Og Mandino

The Millionaire's Treasure Map To Real Estate Investing Success by Dennis J Henson

7 Secrets To Success In Real Estate Investing by Dennis J Henson

Tears of Hope by Aimmee Kodachian

Prison Break; The 9 to 5 Escape Agenda: Taking the Leap from Limitation to Liberation

How to Win Friends and Influence People by Dale Carnegie

Influence by Robert Cialdini

Turning Problems Into Profits

Silver Boxes by Florence Littauer

Reviews (and Feedback) Appreciated

The best way to thank an author is by providing them with feedback on the work they have created. This can come from a review left on Amazon or wherever you purchased the book, or it can come from a short email sent to the author that lets them know what you thought of the work and where you felt it could have been improved or where you felt it really shined.

This feedback is the seed that encourages us to continue writing and helps us to improve our work. We cannot thrive without it. If you're wondering what to say, here's some helpful questions to help you begin:

1. What - specifically - caused you to buy the book?

2. Is there a quote within the book that you found powerful?

3. Did the book live up to the promises it made on the back or in the introduction?

4. If not, where did it fail you?

5. Would you recommend the book to others?

6. If so, why?

7. Were there parts that confused or bored you? If so, what do you think the author could have done better?

8. Were you satisfied with the ending?

9. What did you like most about the book?

10. What did you like least about the book?

11. What do you wish were in the book that you didn't find?

12. What did you find in the book that you wish were not there?

Again, these questions are just places to begin thinking about how to review the work. You do not have to answer all of them or any of them. Feedback can be sent to 40daywriter@gmail.com Subject: RE: Turning Problems Into Profits.

About the Author

Turning Problems Into Profits

Brandy M. Miller is an internationally recognized author, speaker, and trainer who specializes in opportunity prospecting and the cultivation of underdeveloped human beings. Dubbed "relentlessly positive" by William Hung when interviewed for his podcast, she has risen up from poverty, abuse, neglect, abandonment, and homelessness to develop a successful business helping other people find their value and put it down on paper so they can share it with the world.

She lives in Texas with her husband and, when she is not busy helping other people recognize and articulate the value they have to offer others, she enjoys developing games that make learning fun and addictive. Her current project is called WordQuest.Online, a game where users are taught how to write while they are having fun.

She sees writing as ultimately being an adventure of using creativity to think through and solve problems for the world. The game will teach the skills needed to solve problems and write engaging stories around those solutions while allowing the user to practice those skills in a fun, engaging environment.

She intends to use that game to cultivate problem solvers and to connect them with the people who can support them in bringing their solutions to market for the benefit of society.

CONNECT WITH BRANDY ONLINE

Connect with Brandy on her websites:

http://magneticleadershiptraining.com

http://writeyourbook.today

http://wordquest.online

OR BY EMAIL

brandy@40daywriter.com

OR THROUGH HER SOCIAL MEDIA PROFILES

Facebook:

https://www.facebook.com/BrandyMMiller1975

LinkedIn:

https://www.linkedin.com/in/brandymmiller/

Twitter: http://twitter.com/WriterBrandy